THE WORLD CALLING

THE WORLD CALLING
The Church's Witness in Politics and Society

Thomas W. Ogletree

Westminster John Knox Press
LOUISVILLE • LONDON

Chapter 2 is a reprint of Thomas W. Ogletree, "The Public Witness of the Christian Churches: Reflections Based upon Ernst Troeltsch's *Social Teaching of the Christian Churches*" in *Annual of the Society of Christian Ethics* (now known as *Journal of the Society of Christian Ethics*) (1992): 43–74, reprinted with the permission of the coeditor of *Journal of the Society of Christian Ethics*. Chapter 3 is a reprint of Thomas W. Ogletree, "Christian Social Ethics as a Theological Discipline," in *Shifting Boundaries: Contextual Approaches to the Structure of Theological Education*, ed. Barbara G. Wheeler and Edward Farley (Westminster John Knox Press, 1989), 201–39, reprinted with the permission of Westminster John Knox Press. Chapter 4 is a reprint of Thomas W. Ogletree, "Corporate Capitalism and the Common Good: A Framework for Addressing the Challenges of a Global Economy," in *Journal of Religious Ethics* 30, no. 1 (Spring 2002): 79–105, reprinted with the permission of the coeditor of the *Journal of Religious Ethics*. Chapter 5 is a reprint of Thomas W. Ogletree, "Renewing Ecumenical Protestant Social Teaching," in *Justice and the Holy: Essays in Honor of Walter Harrelson*, ed. Douglas Knight and Peter Paris (Scholars Press, 1989), 279–96. Chapter 6 is a reprint of Thomas W. Ogletree, "Faith, Culture, and Power: Reflections on James H. Cone's *Martin & Malcolm & America*," in *Union Seminary Quarterly Review* (March 1995), reprinted with the permission of the editorial staff of *Union Seminary Quarterly Review*. The appendix is a reprint of Thomas W. Ogletree, " 'The Ecclesial Context of Christian Ethics': Presidential Address to the Society of Christian Ethics," in *Annual of the Society of Christian Ethics* (now known as *Journal of the Society of Christian Ethics*) (1983): 1–17, reprinted with the permission of the coeditor of *Journal of the Society of Christian Ethics*.

Book design by Sharon Adams
Cover design by Mark Abrams

First edition
Published by Westminster John Knox Press
Louisville, Kentucky

This book is printed on acid-free paper that meets the American National Standards Institute Z39.48 standard. ♾

PRINTED IN THE UNITED STATES OF AMERICA

04 05 06 07 08 09 10 11 12 13 — 10 9 8 7 6 5 4 3 2 1

Library of Congress Cataloging-in-Publication Data

Ogletree, Thomas W.
    The world calling : the church's witness in politics and society / Thomas W. Ogletree.
    p. cm.
    Includes bibliographical references.
    ISBN 0-664-22874-7 (alk. paper)
    1. Christian sociology—United States. 2. Christianity and politics—United States. 3. Christian sociology—Protestant churches. 4. Christianity and politics—Protestant churches. 5. Protestant churches—United States—Doctrines. I. Title.

    BR517.O35 2004
    261.8—dc22

2004050885

Contents

Preface

*T*his volume is dedicated to the mentors, colleagues, and friends who during the 1960s opened the way for me to become an active participant in the civil rights movement. They released me from deep feelings of guilt over my own entrapment in the racism of American society, and they awakened in me a new confidence that I could make a difference in this world. In important respects, the Reverend Fred Schuttlesworth led the way. As a pastor in my home city, he took bold steps to enroll his adolescent children in the all-white Phillips High School located in downtown Birmingham, Alabama. As I began my studies at Birmingham-Southern College, he awakened in me hopes for changes that would soon come about in our larger society. I am pleased to report that a major thoroughfare in the city of Birmingham now bears his name. Only a few years later, Jim Cone and I became friends while attending seminary together at Garrett Theological Seminary in Evanston, Illinois. We were among a very small number of "southerners" attending seminary in the "Windy City." The prophetic writings that Jim has produced over the course of his highly productive career have served as an inspiration for me and for many, especially for those who long for a transformed world where human beings with all sorts of backgrounds can embrace one another in a wider community of mutual regard and freedom.

The critical turning point in my life took place with the launching of the civil rights movement in Nashville, Tennessee, where I was pursuing PhD studies at Vanderbilt University. Jim Lawson, a fellow Vanderbilt student, stepped forward as the primary trainer for African-American students practicing "civil disobedience" and "nonviolent direct action" by occupying lunch counters and restaurants in downtown Nashville, a city that had been racially segregated throughout its history. The Vanderbilt University Board of Trustees peremptorily expelled Jim Lawson for his leadership in the sit-in movement, fearing outbreaks of violence in response to his activist agenda. The action by the board made clear to me and to my close friend and fellow graduate student Freeman Sleeper that we had to become directly involved in the sit-in movement. We were warmly welcomed by student leaders from Fisk, Tennessee State University, and the National Baptist Seminary. Prominent among these student leaders were Diane Nash, of Fisk University, and John Lewis, of the Baptist Seminary. Several years later, John and I found ourselves standing side by side in the streets of Birmingham as we joined multitudes of mourners at the funeral service for the four little girls who had been killed by a bomb explosion at the Sixteenth Street Baptist Church. By that time, John had already been elected to the U.S. Congress as a Representative from Atlanta, Georgia, a position he continues to hold to this day. Of the experienced pastors in Nashville who worked with student demonstrators, the Rev. C. T. Vivian stands out in my mind. He was a courageous, clear-headed, charismatic leader who empowered and supported me as I anxiously ventured my first self-conscious act of civil disobedience. I shall never forget the way I clung to his coattails as we rushed to take our seats in a legally segregated lunch counter.

My involvements in civil rights issues entered a new stage when I accepted a teaching appointment at the Chicago Theological Seminary (CTS). CTS is located in Hyde Park, the site of the University of Chicago. Jesse Jackson, who had been a student leader of the sit-in movement in South Carolina, had just enrolled as a student at CTS. He had moved to Chicago with the encouragement of Dr. Martin Luther King Jr. to organize "Operation Breadbasket," a program of "nonviolent direct action" designed to press commercial enterprises located in African-American neighborhoods on the south side of Chicago to increase substantially the proportion of their employees who actually lived in those neighborhoods. Companies that did not comply with this demand faced massive boycotts by their customers. With this new initiative, the civil rights movement shifted its focus from the struggle for universal access to public accommodations to demands for increased employment opportunities for people who had been systematically denied those opportunities because of entrenched racial prejudices. Jesse honored me by inviting me to serve on the Advisory Board of Operation Breadbasket. Though I was officially one of Jesse's teachers at CTS, he taught me far more than I could possibly have taught him. On more than one occasion since I began teaching at Yale Divinity School, Jesse and I have crossed paths. He has come to New Haven to offer public support for service unions striving to negotiate more acceptable contracts with Yale University and with other major nonprofit institutions in the city.

It was in the context of my involvements with Operation Breadbasket that I had the privilege of meeting Dr. Martin Luther King Jr. in person. That meeting took place only two years prior to his tragic assassination in Memphis, Tennessee. Operation Breadbasket also gave me the opportunity to observe Andrew Young's extraordinary skills in conflict resolution. He met with a gathering of distinguished pastors and prominent lay leaders, helping them work together more effectively in advancing the cause of Operation Breadbasket. Andy was, of course, a key organizer and manager of activities supported and nurtured by Dr. King. He served as a key official in the administration of President Carter, and he subsequently became the mayor of Atlanta, providing exceptional leadership toward that city's growth and transformation into a major American city.

My debt to these inspiring leaders, mentors, and colleagues is enormous. They have contributed far more to my life than I can ever adequately express. They helped me see that we can make a difference in our world if we have the will to do so. We can foster justice, peace, and the bonds of a greater human community in a world that is persistently distorted by greed, corruption, cruelty, and violence. To be sure, sometimes our most energetic efforts will prove fruitless. Those in positions of power will know how to block and frustrate movements for change that run counter to their interests. We have to learn to discern the times of opportunity when openings emerge that present unprecedented new possibilities for constructive change. At other times, we must learn to practice patient waiting and faithful enduring, holding steadfastly to our deepest convictions even when prospects for constructive change are slim, trusting all the while that God's promises will finally be brought to completion.

The shift in the focus of my academic interests from systematic and philosophical theology to theological ethics, especially Christian social ethics, is one of the enduring outcomes of my earlier involvements in the civil rights movement. I continue to be deeply invested in biblical studies, and in critical reflections on fundamental theological and philosophical matters. Yet I engage these resources chiefly out of a longing to further interfaith and ecumenical Christian engagements with complex social questions, with the hope of fostering a common good that finally accords with God's encompassing purposes for the inhabited earth.

This book is composed of materials that were initially published as independent essays. Because the essays were published separately, their larger systematic connections could not have been clearly manifest. Furthermore, two of the essays—"Christian Social Ethics as a Theological Discipline" and "Renewing Ecumenical Protestant Social Teaching"—appeared in collections that may not have been readily accessible to interested readers. It is my hope that the combination of these materials in a single volume will disclose the unifying vision that underlies them all.

Chapter 2, "The Public Witness of the Christian Churches: Reflections Based upon Ernst Troeltsch's *Social Teaching of the Christian Churches*" (1992) and the Appendix, "The Ecclesial Context of Christian Ethics" (1984) were initially published in *The Annual of the Society of Christian Ethics*. They are incorporated into this volume with the permission of Christine Gudorf and Paul Lauritzen, coeditors of the *Journal of the Society of Christian Ethics*, which is the successor to *The Annual of the Society of Christian Ethics*. Chapter 3, "Christian Social Ethics as a Theological Discipline," initially appeared in *Shifting Boundaries: Contextual Approaches to the Structure of Theological Education*, edited by Barbara G. Wheeler and Edward Farley, and published by Westminster/John Knox Press (1989), which retains the copyright for this chapter. Chapter 4, "Corporate Capitalism and the Common Good: A Framework for Addressing the Challenges of a Global Economy," was initially published in the *Journal of Religious Ethics* (2002). It is reprinted with the permission of the coeditors, John Kelsey and Sumner B. Twiss. Chapter 5, "Renewing Ecumenical Protestant Social Teaching," initially appeared in *Justice and the Holy: Essays in Honor of Walter Harrelson*, edited by Douglas Knight and Peter Paris, and published by Scholars Press (1989). When Scholars Press was closed, copyrights for their published materials reverted to the respective authors. Chapter 6, "Faith, Culture, and Power: Reflections on James H. Cone's *Martin & Malcolm & America*," initially appeared in the *Union Seminary Quarterly Review* (1995). Permission to republish this article in the present book was granted by Jennifer Harvey, *USQR* Editorial Staff.

I want to thank Jack A. Keller, vice president of publishing, Westminster John Knox Press, for his support and his fruitful suggestions regarding the publication of this volume. I am also grateful for his efforts to make three of my earlier books available in an "on-demand" format: *Christian Faith and History: A Critical Comparison of Ernst Troeltsch and Karl Barth*, initially published by Abingdon Press (1965); *The Use of the Bible in Christian Ethics* (1983), and *Hospitality to the Stranger: Dimensions of Moral Understanding* (1985), both of which were initially published by Fortress Press. I now hold the copyrights for these three books.

I want to acknowledge as well the long-term support of many colleagues and friends, in particular, Peter Paris, the late Howard Harrod, Ed Farley, Davis Perkins, Harlan Beckley, Barbara Andolsen, Riggins Earl Jr., Joe Bush, Karen Brown, Patricia Jung, Charles Reynolds, Don Browning, Stan Hauerwas, Bill Schweiker, Jin-Kwan Kwon, Lewis Mudge, Jon Gunneman, Diane Yeager, and also Jack Keller. The contributions that these colleagues have made to my own scholarly work is manifest in multiple ways, some quite subtle, and others obvious and unmistakable. In our quest for understanding, we never walk alone.

Chapter 1

Introduction

Constructing a Christian Social Witness

*T*his volume is devoted to a systematic elaboration of the forms of critical inquiry that are necessary for rendering Christian social teaching effective amid the social and institutional complexities of the contemporary world. Ernst Troeltsch's seminal work, *The Social Teaching of the Christian Churches,*[1] serves as the primary guide for this undertaking. Especially insightful is Troeltsch's insistence on the importance of combining "historical thinking" and "social analysis" in assessing the import of Christian social teaching for evolving societal systems. The title I have chosen for this book reflects a key theme in Troeltsch's account of Protestant contributions to Christian social teaching.[2] In opposition to monastic asceticism, Troeltsch observed, Martin Luther stressed the import of the divine calling for our everyday lives in this transient and fallen world. Our "world calling" is by no means limited to sacral rites and spiritual practices; still less does it entail withdrawal from the world with its established institutions. It encompasses our family relationships, our daily work, our involvements in guilds and professional associations, our duties as citizens, the respect we show for those in authority, and our readiness to perform military service should that become necessary. In short, the divine calling suffuses the whole of our lives, bestowing new levels of meaning upon even the most mundane matters.[3]

John Calvin and his successors embraced Luther's account of our "world calling," stressing its import for *the ways* in which we approach our daily tasks. Our work in the world becomes an occasion for glorifying God, and for attesting the transforming presence of God's grace in our lives. When we

---

1. Troeltsch, Ernst, *The Social Teaching of the Christian Churches,* 2 vol., trans. Olive Wyon (Louisville, Ky.: Westminster/John Knox Press, 1992).
2. Cf. vol. 2, pp. 461–655.
3. Ibid., 472–73.

approach our work with these understandings, we invest new levels of diligence and discipline toward achieving the highest possible levels of performance in everything that we do. Drawing upon the work of Max Weber, Troeltsch directed particular attention to the contributions that Calvinism and Puritanism have made toward the rise of capitalism and the formation of modern democratic states.[4] In both spheres, the Reformation traditions have provided a vitally important paradigm for the social, economic, and political responsibilities of contemporary Christians, especially for those living in democratic societies with free-market economies.

The primary challenge in our present day is to equip Christians with a clearer vision of their social and political obligations in a religiously and culturally diverse setting where public expressions of religious sensibilities often appear inappropriate. Closely related is the challenge of sustaining and also renewing substantive moral standards that are themselves requisite for the full functioning of these modern societal systems. To serve the American churches, especially in a post–Cold War global economy, Troeltsch's inquiries require substantial development, even transformation. Nonetheless, for studies in Christian social ethics, including current attempts to rethink the public vocation of the Christian churches, his basic insights remain virtually indispensable.

To begin with, Troeltsch underscored the fact that the societal arrangements that order human affairs in various social and historical settings are constituted both by organizational principles and substantive moral values whose operations remain independent of distinctively Christian teachings. There is, in other words, no such thing as a Christian civilization, nor can social ideas grounded in the Christian message be directly applied within established social institutions. Christian commitments to foster human well-being within the ongoing practices of an existing social order require theological grounds, what Troeltsch called a comprehensive "doctrine of civilization." The purpose of such a doctrine is to make clear what roles Christians can properly play in an alien social world while also sustaining their foundational commitments to the transforming promises of the Christian message.

Second, a credible civilizational doctrine must include a critical analysis of the actual operations of particular societal systems. What are the basic structures and functional dynamics that facilitate collaborative human practices

---

4. Cf. Max Weber, *The Protestant Ethic and the Spirit of Capitalism*, trans. Talcott Parsons (New York: Scribner, 1956). On Calvinism and democracy, cf. Troeltsch, pp. 628–41. On Calvinism and Capitalism, cf. Troeltsch, pp. 641–50.

within a given social order? To take a specific example, what are the economic, social, and cultural conditions that render democratic governments feasible? Why has democracy generally worked well in the United States? Why does it appear so elusive in Russia, or Serbia, or Pakistan, or China, or the Congo? Even more challenging is the task of determining the social requisites of fully functioning market economies, not simply within national boundaries but within an expanding global arena where international financial institutions and trade organizations play indispensable roles.

Societal systems equally require for their viability widely recognized moral standards and substantive moral values. Troeltsch referred to these standards and values as a society's civilizational ethic, for they regulate and guide ongoing human practices within a given society. To enjoy authority, these standards must themselves be fully integrated with the basic structures and operational dynamics that give order to that society. Otherwise, they amount to little more than ideological cover utilized by ruling powers to conceal from a wider citizenry existing social and political realities. Particular societal systems invariably privilege certain value sets over others. Societies with free-market economies, for example, generally place higher value upon efficiency, productivity, and aggregate economic growth than upon fairness in the distribution of income and wealth. Socialist states in contrast favor basic material security for all citizens, even at the cost of economic stagnation and bureaucratic inefficiency. In well-ordered societies, basic moral standards and substantive moral values are explicit ingredients in the common culture, and they are routinely internalized in the socialization processes that contribute to personal formation. Central elements in the civilizational ethic will also be sanctioned in public law, with coercive police and criminal procedures to deal with those who violate or disregard the law. Troeltsch's basic contention is that Christian social teaching must be pertinent to specific forms of social organization in order to become effective in practice. Consequently, it must be informed by critical social theory, theory that encompasses complex social, cultural, economic, and political processes in their distinctions and interrelationships.

The third major task in the generation of credible bodies of Christian social teaching is pivotal. It is to assemble and to articulate explicit social ideas that appear to be resident in the Christian message itself. In effect, we are seeking to discern in the Christian story anticipatory worldly manifestations of promises that manifest God's ultimate purposes for the world, even though those promises will be fully realized only in the final consummation of God's coming realm. The critical retrieval of formative traditions of social teaching takes on special importance because the biblical witness and substantive appropriations of that witness within the churches have themselves emerged over extended histories embracing multiple adjustments and adaptations within shifting patterns of social organization. In the course of Western history, moreover, Christian churches have experienced strikingly different placements within evolving social systems. They have been subjected to persecution as marginal communities that were judged to be threats to stability and social order, and they have been closely linked to centers of political power as bearers of an official state religion. Social and historical readings of formative Christian traditions alert us to the complexities and ambiguities of conscientious efforts to formulate an authentic social message. These efforts have resulted in distortions, even betrayals, of distinctively Christian understandings; yet they have also contributed substantially to human well-being, even within the constraints of a sinful and fallen world. If we are to reclaim and renew formative traditions of Christian social teaching, we require an ecclesial setting for our deliberations, where persons of faith are striving to discern their worldly vocations. We invariably confront the transient and flawed nature of a sinful social world, but we also acknowledge with gratitude God's providential sustenance of a fallen world as an arena within which we can pursue our lifelong journeys in faith.

The next challenge is to discover constructive ways of relating distinctively Christian social ideas to the civilizational ethic resident in a given social order. The underlying claim is that normative social teachings, Christian or otherwise, cannot become socially effective unless they can be rendered compatible with the organizational principles that structure particular societies. What is possible in one setting may be wholly unrealistic in another. The attainment of such compatibility requires a "cultural synthesis," that is, a creative combination of distinctively Christian values with core elements in a reigning "civilizational ethic." In the American context, for example, the quest for a viable synthesis necessarily involves giving privileged standing to the "blessings of liberty" celebrated in the Preamble to the U.S. Constitution. The First Amendment lifts up the foundational liberties: free expression of religion, free speech, free press, free assembly, and the right to petition the government on matters of concern. In the American setting, a credible body of Christian social teaching must fully embrace these liberties in a clear and unequivocal manner.

Troeltsch was convinced that a workable "cultural synthesis" would necessarily involve compromises, that is, some accommodation of Christian understandings to existing social realities. The search for viable compromises can, of course, subvert the Christian message itself, perhaps by integrating it with morally reprehensible social practices, such as Christian sanctions for chattel slavery in southern states of the U.S. Federal Republic prior to the Civil War, or "German Christian" endorsements of Naziism. Even minimal attempts to survive in a sinful social world require compromises of some sort. Yet the cultural synthesis of which Troeltsch speaks is not primarily addressed to issues of bare survival; it rather concerns prospects for a transforming Christian social presence, a presence that can attest God's righteous purposes even within the constraints of a sinful world. In contrast, a principled refusal of all possible compromises could amount to a stance of passivity or timidity in the presence of grave social injustices and widespread human suffering. The enduring challenge to Christian fidelity is to resist compromises that distort the Christian message while boldly venturing compromises that can facilitate legitimate and fruitful contributions to more just and humane forms of social order.

Troeltsch's call for a credible "cultural synthesis" rests upon the judgment that socially pertinent moral standards must in any case be congruent with the organizational principles of specific societies. While this judgment does not explicitly entail any repudiation of attempts to formulate universal moral principles based upon compelling rational arguments, it does underscore the abstractness of such undertakings. Contemporary debates about Human Rights display this reality. In the U.S. context, the priority given to productivity and efficiency by private enterprises and profit-making corporations within a free-market economy renders unpersuasive articles in the Bill of human rights that deal with economic rights. At the same time, the U.S. Constitution treats as self-evident rights associated with personal freedoms and civil liberties. In contrast, highly centralized, authoritarian states are disposed to consider personal and civil liberties as at best socially destabilizing and, potentially, even subversive. Within limits, however, such states may be willing to acknowledge basic claims about economic rights, the rights of human beings to the material requisites of existence. In other words, attempts to construct universal and rationally grounded moral principles can take on practical importance only insofar as those principles can themselves be integrated with a reigning civilizational ethic, one that is fully congruent with an established system of societal order.

The final task necessary for credible bodies of Christian social teachings is to devise practical strategies for promoting such teachings and for implementing their pivotal values within the ongoing operations of existing human societies. Troeltsch gave virtually no attention to this undertaking, in part because the rapid rise in Europe of highly centralized national states appeared to render irrelevant classic bodies of Christian social teaching, except to the degree that values derived from such teaching had already become more or less stable components of a broader European culture. Yet strategic questions remain vital to the social witness of American churches, in part because democratic institutions protect substantial space both for individual initiatives and also for the public activities of voluntary associations and organizations that have been formed precisely to advance specific social causes.

Strategic interests have multiple dimensions of their own. They require sustained attention to specific arenas of public policy. With regard to a particular social concern, what policies are already in place? How well are they working? Are they achieving their desired objectives, or are they producing unintended negative consequences? We cannot remain content, that is to say, merely with general statements of ethical principles, for example, a constructive theory of justice. We must also concern ourselves with assessing the levels of justice that have actually been achieved as a result of particular social policies. Studies in policy ethics present enormous challenges, in part because policy issues are debated and implemented in multiple contexts. They involve legislative processes at various levels of government, and they encompass discretionary administrative practices devised and enforced by a complex array of governmental departments and agencies. State and federal courts frequently play crucial roles in these processes as well. Among other things, policy studies heighten our awareness of the degree to which serious social problems are simply ignored or perhaps dismissed by many of the nation's political leaders. The society's most vulnerable members are rarely able to gain an effective public voice. The prophetic witness of the churches embraces attempts to heighten public awareness about social injustices that urgently call for collective action.

Second, attention to strategic issues in Christian social teaching brings to the fore fundamental questions about the appropriateness of church involvements in the public life of a democracy, especially one that prohibits any form of religious establishment and rigorously protects the free exercise of religion. Advocates for a public witness by Christian churches must be attentive to these issues. They must be able to demonstrate that a public witness arising out of the ministries of Christian churches can be pursued in a fashion that is fully compatible with America's civilizational ethic. They must also be able to show that such a witness can contribute to the greater human good, both in the United States and in the wider world.

The third set of issues concerns the appropriate organizational arenas for advancing Christian social teaching both within the churches and within a wider society. For the Roman Catholic Church, the primary responsibilities for delineating Christian social teaching reside in the teaching authority of the Pope; in the pronouncements of official conciliar bodies, such as Vatican II;

and in pastoral letters delivered by national or regional gatherings of Catholic bishops. Of singular importance are the papal social encyclicals, beginning with *Rerum Novarum* in 1891, and embracing the multiple encyclicals of Pope John Paul II during the course of his extended tenure. For the most part, official Roman Catholic social teachings have been restricted to general principles of justice and fairness as they apply to established social arenas. While these principles usually reflect given forms of social organization, they intentionally remain a step removed from more substantive policy debates. However, with respect to what are judged to be core moral standards, U.S. Catholic bishops, with firm backing by the Pope, have aggressively promoted the implementation in public law of particular Roman Catholic moral teachings. The matters of primary concern are well known: the legal prohibition of abortions and of all forms of stem cell research; active resistance to any legal recognition for gay and lesbian civil unions, and above all, for marriages between persons of the same gender; and finally, the termination of publicly funded programs to distribute contraceptive devices as means for reducing unwanted pregnancies. Conservative evangelical Protestant political organizations are equally aggressive in fighting for these standards.

Given the prominence accorded to lay consent within Protestant understandings of the church's teaching authority, official denominational, ecumenical, and interfaith organizations are far more limited in what they can actively advocate in regard to Christian social teachings. Denominational and ecumenical Protestant assemblies can and do debate and act upon resolutions that address particular public issues. They also form study commissions to pursue more detailed investigations of specific matters of concern, drawing on the professional expertise of lay members. Similarly, some denominations maintain national agencies to see that publicly active church members remain fully informed about the current status of vitally important legislative matters under consideration at state and federal levels. Finally, councils of bishops within selected Protestant denominations—Episcopal, Lutheran, Methodist—may in the exercise of their pastoral authority generate critical studies of major public issues. Strictly speaking, normative standards and values articulated in these various Protestant arenas do not constitute authoritative bodies of Christian social teaching. They rather serve as resources for study and reflection within the ongoing ministries of individual congregations. They hold special value for active participants in independent voluntary associations formed to advance Christian social teaching in the public life of the nation.

For the most part, practical Christian initiatives to address particular political issues, whether Catholic or Protestant, require organizing activities by independent associations of concerned citizens, sometimes with and sometimes without explicit denominational, ecumenical, or interfaith identifications. Indeed, in a society marked by multiple religious bodies, cooperative endeavors among diverse groups take on vital importance. Underlying all of these possibilities are efforts by individual congregations, denominations, and ecumenical and interfaith organizations to foster outreach ministries into surrounding neighborhoods, ministries that exemplify basic Christian social teachings. Examples include organized commitments to community renewal, or emergency services for those in desperate need—homeless shelters, soup kitchens, basic health-care services, and spiritual nurture for those who are sick or in prison.

Given the complexities of modern social worlds, it should be quite clear that credible bodies of Christian social teaching cannot easily be articulated and implemented within public arenas. This volume does not by any means address all of the relevant concerns. It represents a constructive attempt to shed more light on crucial aspects of a much larger undertaking, setting the stage for continuing research and inquiry. Furthermore, it primarily reflects the practices of ecumenical Protestant denominations; yet I believe that the issues it addresses also have pertinence for Roman Catholic social teachings and for the public witness of conservative evangelical Protestant churches. The central conviction informing the work as a whole is that concerns for justice and human well-being are integral components of Christian fidelity. While we are undoubtedly limited in what we can realistically achieve in a sinful and fallen world, we remain obligated to do what is in our power. Our calling in Christ energizes us to undertake this task.

Chapter 2, "The Public Witness of the Christian Churches," provides an overview of Ernst Troeltsch's constructive approach to Christian social teaching, with emphasis on the continuing pertinence of his work for the contemporary American setting. Chapter 3, "Christian Social Ethics as a Theological Discipline," addresses the placement of social-ethical inquiries within a more comprehensive account of theological study. It elaborates some of the methodological procedures identified in chapters 1 and 2. Chapter 4, "Corporate Capitalism and the Common Good," applies the method outlined in the first three chapters of the book to an assessment of the role that the federal government must play in both constituting and overseeing a free-market economy. While imprudent policies can jeopardize a free-market economy, the government still plays an indispensable role in assuring that such an economy functions effectively, and that it serves the common good. This chapter also stresses the impact on domestic economies of an expanding global economy, though it does not elaborate the broader ramifications of such an economy for human well-being throughout the world.

The next two chapters highlight the mission of the churches in fostering and sustaining Christian social teaching. Chapter 5, "Renewing Ecumenical Protestant Social Teaching," calls attention to the difficulties that clerical leaders in ecumenical Protestant churches encounter when they find themselves summoned to offer a social witness that exceeds a broadly established lay consensus regarding the churches's proper mission. Two cases are considered: 1) the decision by key church officials in predominately "white" denominations both to endorse and to participate actively in the civil rights movement led by Dr. Martin Luther King Jr.; and 2) similar public involvements by prominent church officials in the anti–Vietnam War movement. In both instances clerical leaders acted without lay authorization or consent, thereby provoking a "gathering storm" in the churches. These cases underscore the importance of fostering authentically Christian social teaching at all levels of church life. They also remind us that a faithful prophetic witness can have substantial costs, both personal and organizational.

Chapter 6, "Faith, Culture, and Power," draws upon James H. Cone's impressive study, *Martin & Malcolm & America: A Dream or A Nightmare,*[5] to dramatize the contributions that distinctively African-American faith communities, both Christian and Muslim, have made and continue to make toward struggles for social justice within American society. Cone highlights important dimensions of social-ethical inquiry that emerge in the teachings of Dr. King and Malcolm X. Four themes stand out: a) an effective prophetic witness must be practice based; b) it must have firm grounding in formative faith traditions; c) it must be attentive to the ways in which social and cultural dynamics both shape and distort human perceptions of the world; and d) it must take account of ways in which organizational and institutional structures impact efforts to generate movements for social change. These structures invariably present formidable barriers to liberating initiatives; at the same time, they furnish indispensable resources for effective public action. The challenge is to find innovative ways of redirecting established social practices toward new ways of living and thinking. What fascinates me about Cone's book is the fact that these themes pervade his discussion even though they do not as such constitute the central focus of his study. Cone helps us see how the leadership offered by Martin and Malcolm provide models of enduring importance for Christian social teaching. These models have pertinence for the public contributions of all vital religious communities operating in the context of American democratic institutions.

---

5. Cone, James H., *Martin & Malcolm & America: A Dream or a Nightmare* (Maryknoll, NY: Orbis Books, 1991).

Finally, I have included an appendix that contains my presidential address to the Society of Christian Ethics, "The Ecclesial Context of Christian Ethics" (1984). While this address focuses considerable attention on the ongoing work of the society, it stresses the importance of the worldly mission of the churches for all aspects of theological ethical inquiry. It also underscores the difficulties of forming and sustaining communities that can foster Christian ethical teachings, especially in their import for the wider social world. In both respects, therefore, it reinforces and expands materials treated in chapters 5 and 6.

Chapter 2

The Public Witness of the Christian Churches

Reflections Based upon Ernst Troeltsch's *Social Teaching of the Christian Churches*

*D*o Christian churches have something to say to urgent social problems in contemporary America, or indeed, in a wider global community? More precisely, do they have a substantive role to play in the formation of public policies that bear upon such problems?

In general, students of Christian social ethics take for granted an affirmative answer to these questions. They are deeply invested in examining the great social questions of our day, and they aspire to propose appropriate Christian responses. They see this task as integral to a faithful hearing of the Gospel. At the same time, the actual attempts of church leaders to address public issues have become quite problematic in recent years, compelling a reexamination of what a Christian witness entails.

I want to look critically at the presumptions underlying the belief that the churches have something to say to contemporary social problems. In this undertaking I shall draw upon Ernst Troeltsch's master work, *The Social Teaching of the Christian Churches*.[1] My intent is to suggest ways of refining studies in Christian social ethics to take fuller account of how social and cultural realities qualify the possibilities for an effective Christian witness.

I. Presumptions Underlying a Christian Social Witness

What do we take for granted when we advocate a Christian social witness? What are our crucial assumptions? There are four central ideas.

First, a Christian social witness presumes that the Gospel contains social convictions that have normative import for the organization and development of human societies.

---

1. Ernst Troeltsch, *The Social Teaching of the Christian Churches*, trans. Olive Wyon with a Foreword by James Luther Adams (Louisville, KY: Westminster/John Knox Press, 1992).

Second, a Christian social witness presumes that the organizational principles that structure the basic institutions of human societies are amenable to shaping by Christian social convictions.

Third, a Christian social witness presumes that Christian social convictions have legitimate authority in the public discourse of human societies. This presumption is relatively straightforward in societies that have an established church. It becomes more complex and controversial in secular, religiously plural societies, especially those that constitutionally prohibit any religious establishment.

Fourth, a Christian social witness presumes that there is an authoritative account of Christian social convictions that is broadly recognized and affirmed by the membership of the churches.

Troeltsch investigated the first and second of these two presumptions at length. The latter two take on special importance in the American setting. Hence, they did not figure in his studies. Nonetheless, as I hope to make clear, his methods of inquiry and his controlling concepts provide suggestions for dealing with these latter considerations as well.

II. Troeltsch's Project in the *Social Teaching*

Troeltsch's study of Christian social teaching was motivated throughout by constructive interests. Writing in the midst of European social, economic, and political ferment, he sought ways of assessing the efforts of church leaders to develop Christian views of society and to propose Christian responses to overwhelming social problems. He had two overarching questions. First, he wanted to know whether it is theologically appropriate to undertake Christian social teaching, and if so, what the churches' attitude had been and now ought to be toward modern social problems. Second, he wanted to know what the churches had achieved in practice with regard to social reform, and whether their previous achievements offered something valuable for the modern situation.[2]

Broadly speaking, the results of Troeltsch's inquiries were largely negative. Though he was able to identify distinctively Christian traditions of social thought that had previously enjoyed considerable influence in European civ-

---

2. Ibid., 23–24, 34. In this respect, it is a mistake to read Troeltsch simply as a historian of Christian ethics, still less, as a sociologist of religion who formulated an interesting typology of the churches' organizational expressions. He was preeminently a Christian theologian with a special interest in the churches' social witness. He was a historian and a sociologist because he believed that an adequate critical understanding of the churches' social message required historical thinking and social analysis, both functioning as indispensable resources in the critical mediation of the churches' normative teaching.

ilization, he did not see that any of those traditions held noteworthy promise for the modem situation. He concluded that the churches were not likely to play a formative role in the future evolution of European societies, except perhaps through a residue of Christian ideas that had become integral features of a broader European civilizational ethic. He later called that ethic "Europeanism."[3] In this respect, his thought took a turn comparable to the recent embrace of civil religion within the American context.[4] When Europeanism or the American civil religion furnish the normative center of social thought, then it is not clear that Christian social ethics as such has any more role to play. It gives way to public ethics or civilizational ethics, or perhaps to public theology.[5] The distinctively Christian task, then, is simply to determine the grounds for legitimate Christian participation in a public arena whose governing norms are independent of, even alien to, the Gospel message.[6]

By the beginning of the twentieth century, Troeltsch believed, Christian ideas had largely lost their civilizational import. Their enduring significance, if any, was limited to the private lives of individual Christians, where maximum freedom could be granted for the expression of personal preferences.

3. See Ernst Troeltsch, *Der Historismus und seine Probleme*, Book I, *Das Logische Problem der Geschichtsphilosophie, vol. 3, Gesammelte Schriften* (Tübingen: Scientia Verlag Aalen, 1977), 703–30.

4. Robert Bellah crystallized interest in an American civil religion. See his *The Broken Covenant* (New York: Seabury Press, 1975). See also Robert Bellah and Phillip Hammond, *Varieties of Civil Religion* (San Francisco: Harper and Row, 1980).

5. Over the last decade, studies dealing with the American civil religion, public theology, and public ethics have multiplied. Some representative studies include John A. Coleman, *An American Strategic Theology* (New York: Paulist Press, 1982); Charles Davis, *Theology and Political Society* (Cambridge, England: Cambridge University Press, 1980); Franklin I. Gamwell, *The Divine Good: Modern Moral Theory and the Necessity of God* (San Francisco: Harper Collins Publishers, 1990); Ralph Ketcham, *Individualism and Public Life* (New York: Basil Blackwell, 1987); Robin Lovin, ed., *Religion and American Public Life* (New York: Paulist Press, 1986); Dennis P. McCann and Charles R. Strain, *Polity and Praxis: A Program for American Practical Theology* (Minneapolis: Winston, 1985); Richard John Neuhaus, *The Naked Public Square: Religion and Democracy in America* (Grand Rapids, MI: Eerdmans, 1984); Parker J. Palmer, *The Company of Strangers: Christians and the Renewal of America's Public Life* (New York: Crossroad, 1982); Leroy S. Rouner, ed., *Civil Religion and Political Theology* (South Bend, IN: University of Notre Dame Press, 1986); Max Stackhouse, *Public Theology and Political Economy: Christian Stewardship in Modern Society* (Grand Rapids, MI: Eerdmans, 1987; reprint, Lanham, MD: University Press of America, 1991); and Jeffrey Stout, *Ethics After Babel* (Boston: Beacon Press, 1988). Three older studies are William Coats, *God in Public: Political Theology Beyond Niebuhr* (Grand Rapids, MI: Eerdmans, 1974); James Sellers, *Public Ethics* (New York: Macmillan, 1970); and Gibson Winter, *Elements for a Social Ethics: Scientific and Ethical Perspectives on Social Process* (New York: Macmillan, 1966).

For studies in social and political theory that have relevance for the discussion, see Mary Ann Glendon, *Rights Talk: The Impoverishment of Political Discourse* (New York: The Free Press, 1991); Thomas E. McCollough, *The Moral Imagination and Public Life* (Chatham, NJ: Chatham House Publishers, Inc., 1991); Richard Sennett, *The Fall of Public Man* (New York: Knopf, 1977); and William M. Sullivan, *Reconstructing Public Philosophy* (Los Angeles: University of California Press, 1986).

6. This focus accords with a central Reformation tradition. See such classics as Emil Brunner, *The Divine Imperative,* trans. Olive Wyon (Philadelphia: The Westminster Press, 1937), 198–233, or Dietrich

Troeltsch labeled such individualistic and privatistic appropriations of the Christian faith "mysticism," stressing the personal, inward, and experiential features of religious consciousness over against its corporate, sacramental, and institutional elements. These latter forms of piety allow room, he argued, only for the weakest and most unstable of organizational patterns, that is, the voluntary association of like-minded individuals. Such associations, he believed, are incapable of substantial social impact.

III. Social Ideas and Christian Origins

A. The Religious Nature of the Primitive Christian Message

Troeltsch began his investigations with a fresh look at historical reconstructions of Christian origins. On the basis of these studies, he challenged the presumption that the Christian Gospel contained a socio-political vision concerned with the organization, development, and transformation of human society. The earliest Christian movement, he argued, was not a social movement at all, at least not in the modern sense. It was a religious movement.[7]

In its primitive articulations, Troeltsch argued, the Christian message did not even invite the attempt to undertake a critical analysis of the social, economic, or political causes of human suffering in the first-century Roman world. Still less did it suggest a conception of the social good that might guide a sociopolitical movement seeking the transformation and reconstruction of the social order. It was throughout preoccupied with essentially religious interests. It centered on the ultimate purposes of God in the creation and redemption of the world, and on the formation and sustenance of communities living faithfully and obediently as the people of God in the midst of a fallen world. In relation to these interests, social and political realities remained quite secondary.

To be sure, the early Christian movement reflected social conditions in Palestine and the wider Roman world. Its spread was facilitated and shaped by surrounding socio-political realities. Even as a religious movement it unquestionably had social and political ramifications. Indeed, any movement that attracts a wide following and releases high levels of energy will have an impact on established social institutions.

Bonhoeffer, *Ethics* (New York: Macmillan, 1955), 194–230, 254–258. Concepts such as the "orders" and the "office" in Brunner, and the "mandates," "deputyship," and the "responsible life" in Bonhoeffer, serve to interpret the nature and limits of Christian social involvements.

7. Troeltsch said "purely religious," surely an overstatement since nothing historical is ever purely anything. See *Social Teaching*, 39, 40, 42, 48, 50.

For this reason, Roman governors in Palestine were disposed to nip in the bud grass roots movements of any kind, lest they set processes in motion that might subsequently present serious political problems. Pilate's decision to order Jesus' crucifixion, in other words, did not require a judgment that Jesus had a subversive political agenda; it only required evidence that Jesus stirred up the people, and hence, created a potentially explosive social situation.[8]

It is anachronistic, Troeltsch contended, to read contemporary social concerns back into the message of Jesus. The available evidence simply does not support such attempts. Insofar as there is a distinctive Christian social witness, that witness is a subsequent development, the historical emergence of a particular way of unfolding the import of the earliest Christian proclamation. More recent studies of the social world of early Christianity have not given us reason to alter Troeltsch's assessment.[9]

B. Social Ideas Associated with the Christian Message

Troeltsch did find in the earliest Christian teaching some important social ideas that were intimately associated with the Gospel. These ideas had considerable import for the internal life of the fledgling communities of faith. Troeltsch noted such things as: a) the renunciation of violence and of established judicial processes as means of resolving internal community disputes; b) a stress on patience, forbearance, and mutual forgiveness as ways of sustaining communal bonds; c) the relative disregard for economic security or political power in favor of faithful and trusting allegiance to God's coming realm; d) the sharing of material resources for the well-being of community

8. The argument was presented in an unpublished lecture by Rebecca Gray at the Yale Divinity School, December 1991, entitled "The Crucifixion of Jesus." The writings of Josephus provided her principal ancient source.

9. See *Social Teaching,* 42.

A convenient summary of some of the main results of recent scholarship on the social setting of early Christianity is provided by John E. Stambaugh and David L. Balch, *The New Testament in Its Social Environment* (Philadelphia: The Westminster Press, 1986). I have found especially helpful Gerd Theissen's studies, *Sociology of Early Palestinian Christianity,* trans. by John Schutz (Philadelphia: Fortress Press, 1978); *The Social Setting of Pauline Christianity,* (Philadelphia: Fortress Press, 1982); and most recently, *The Gospels in Context: Social and Political Tradition in the Synoptic Tradition* (Philadelphia: Fortress Press, 1991). See also Wayne Meeks, *The First Urban Christians* (New Haven: Yale University Press, 1983) and E. P. Sanders, *Jesus and Judaism* (Philadelphia: Fortress Press, 1985).

For recent attempts to portray Jesus as a social reformer, see Richard Horsley, *Jesus and the Spiral of Violence: Popular Jewish Resistance in Roman Palestine* (San Francisco: Harper & Row, 1987) and Marcus Borg, *Jesus, A New Vision: Spirit, Culture, and the Life of Discipleship* (San Francisco: Harper & Row, 1987). For a thorough-going critique of these efforts, see E. P. Sanders's 1991 Shaffer Lectures at Yale Divinity School, "Jesus: Religious Type and Cause of Death in Recent Interpretation," summarized in *Reflections,* 87, no. 1 (Winter-Spring, 1992): 4–12. *Reflections* is a publication of Yale Divinity School.

members.[10] To Troeltsch's list I would add the breakdown of hierarchical leadership structures in favor of more diverse and fluid charismatic patterns, and the celebration of an inclusive community of equals in Jesus Christ, one that transcended distinctions of culture, ethnicity, gender, and class.[11]

Troeltsch recognized that ideas such as these furnished fertile resources for generating a broader social vision. They did not initially serve, however, as resources for that more complex task. Rather, their purpose was to order the internal life of the Christian communities. These emergent communities believed that they constituted a new people of God in faith, hope, and love. Yet they knew that they had to sustain themselves and carry out their evangelizing mission in a social order whose basic structures and processes remained external to their life and beyond their effective reach. Rather than striving to transform the social world, the earliest Christians sought appropriate ways to protect and advance their shared commitments within an essentially alien social environment.

C. Individualism and Universalism:
The Dialectical Structure of the Christian Message

For Troeltsch, the internal dynamics of the Christian message were actually more important for subsequent social thought than were the specific social ideas associated with that message. The dynamics he had in view were those generated by the dialectical interplay within the Gospel itself of ideas of "absolute individualism" and "absolute universalism."[12]

For Troeltsch, individualism and universalism were but two facets of one

10. *Social Teaching*, 60, 62.

11. See my *The Use of the Bible in Christian Ethics* (Philadelphia: Fortress Press, 1983), 116–127, 129–130. See also my essay, "The Eschatological Horizon of New Testament Social Thought," *Hospitality to the Stranger: Dimensions of Moral Experience* (Philadelphia: Fortress Press, 1985), 127–149.

12. See *Social Teaching*, 55–58. Note that Troeltsch uses neither of these terms in ways common to contemporary discourse. Individualism does not connote isolated individuals. The individuals who respond to the Gospel are not simply wrenched loose from established institutional arrangements; they are simultaneously drawn into strong new communities. The latter become determinative for their lives. Thus, what is individualistic with respect to the basic institutions of society is communitarian in its concrete reality.

Likewise, universalism does not refer to a radical transcendence of historical determinateness that renders the claims of the Gospel immediately binding for all persons in all times and places. Universalism is not an a priori possession of rational beings, nor does it consist in an abstract imperative to reconceive the Gospel message in terms of universally valid principles. It rather concerns the recognition in faith of the solidarity of all creatures in "the holy divine will of love." See ibid., 57. As a historical project, universalism is principally an object of hope and an imperative to faithful discipleship, both arising from the redemptive action of God in Jesus Christ. A universal human community can gain concrete reality, if at all, only in the course of history where the Christian message takes root in a multiplicity of social settings according to a multiplicity of cultural forms.

and the same reality. Both sprang from a common religious root. On the one hand, the Gospel addressed persons as individuals. It wrenched them loose from all prior social connections. In so doing, it rendered irrelevant all the normal distinctions that divide human beings: nationality, race, gender, class. Yet the individualism of the Gospel also contained a strong idea of fellowship. As individuals gave up old patterns of social existence, they were free to enter vital new communal associations where they experienced the transforming power of God's Spirit in a fellowship of love and mutual affirmation.

On the other hand, in binding individuals to God in faith, the Gospel had universal import. Within the unity of God's love, individual differences among human beings gave way to a common recognition of need, a mutual readiness to forgive, and a shared commitment to renounce sin and to join the fight against evil. In a strict sense, Troeltsch noted, this recognition of human solidarity extended no further than the reach of explicit Christian belief. It was not equivalent, therefore, to a general humanitarian ideal. Nonetheless, it furnished the driving energy for the missionary expansion of Christianity, and it sustained hope, courage, and joyfulness where this mission encountered resistance or failed.

Because of the individualism-universalism dialectic, Troeltsch observed, the earliest Christian teaching had both radical and conservative tendencies. The individualism of the Gospel had the effect of weakening existing social institutions. It exposed the hollowness of their pretentions to permanence, and undermined the authority of their regulative principles. In so doing, it fostered a communal environment favorable to radical social criticism.

The universalism of the Gospel disposed the faithful to honor established social structures, for those structures sustained an ordered world that made human life possible. Despite their ambiguity and transiency, they served as instruments of God's sovereign lordship over a sinful and fallen world. So far as possible, Christians adjusted their activities to the institutional constraints necessary for social existence. "Be subject to the governing authorities," Paul admonished Christians in Rome, "for there is no authority except from God, and those that exist have been instituted by God" (Rom. 13.1).[13]

This dual response to the basic institutions of society, Troeltsch argued, has

---

13. See *Social Teaching*, 82–86. I have expressed this dialectic as an eschatological dialectic, in part to avoid the misleading connotations of Troeltsch's terms. The eschatological dialectic concerns the tension between the presence of the coming new age of God and the providential persistence of the old age that is passing away. Christians are to be in the new age in a fashion that also embraces appropriate recognition for the continuing role of the old within the economy of God's purposes. See *The Use of the Bible in Christian Ethics*, 177–192. See also "The Eschatological Horizon of New Testament Social Thought," in *Hospitality to the Stranger*, 141–145.

characterized Christian thought throughout the centuries. Indeed, the individualism-universalism dialectic displays the normative basis of Troeltsch's well-known church-sect typology. The sect is an organizational form that preserves the individualism (and communalism) of the Gospel, but has tended to lose its universalism. The church is an organizational form that normally preserves the universalism of the Gospel, but tends to lose its individualism. The church type enjoyed primacy in Troeltsch's analysis since it constituted stability and continuity for Christian life. Yet it repeatedly required correction and renewal through the stimulus of sectarian movements. As Troeltsch saw it, the challenge to ecclesiastical organization is to embrace church-type and sect-type tendencies, preserving the integrity of the individualism-universalism dialectic.[14]

To summarize, Troeltsch rejected claims that the earliest Christian message contained a social witness in the modern sense. It reflected and responded to social realities, but it offered no systematic social critique nor any concrete program for social reconstruction. The social ideas that were generated by this message chiefly concerned the ordered life of newly established communities of faith. These ideas had virtually no bearing on basic social institutions, for which the earliest Christians had little or no responsibility.

Even so, primitive Christian teaching contained resources that might under different circumstances be elaborated as a pertinent social message. Especially important in this connection was the individualism-universalism dialectic that expressed the central dynamism of the Gospel. Troeltsch's project was to trace the churches' use of these primitive resources in articulating a social message.

IV. Social Institutions and Christian Influences

A. The Normative Independence of Social Institutions

Regarding the second presumption, Troeltsch argued that the basic institutions of human societies are not intrinsically amenable to shaping by Christian teaching. Economic and political institutions in particular, he contended,

---

14. Troeltsch did not use the church-sect typology in a sociologically descriptive way. His interest was normative, an attempt to identify those organizational expressions that are appropriate to the Christian message. The typology itself grew out of Troeltsch's most elemental grasp of the import of the Christian gospel. In this connection, the church-sect typology was not used to describe the earliest Christian movement, except retrospectively. The typology was introduced only at the end of the study of medieval Christendom, to prepare the way for an analysis of the Protestant Reformation. See *Social Teaching*, 340–342.

operate by "organizational principles" that are fundamentally independent of the Christian message.[15] They have not emerged as vehicles of a Christian social vision, and they function with quite different interests, for example, the production and distribution of income and wealth, or the maintenance of public order, to name only the most obvious matters. Basic social institutions, moreover, invariably contain normative understandings that are internal to their operation. These understandings constitute what Troeltsch called a society's "civilizational ethic." The civilizational ethic defines the purposes of various institutional arrangements, and it specifies the activities and patterns of interaction that are expected of those who participate in them.

If we are to offer a Christian social vision, Troeltsch contended, we cannot ignore the actual functioning of the social world. We certainly cannot simply apply any set of social ideas we happen to find compelling to any institutional realities whatever. To gain pertinence, normative social ideas must have a substantive fit with social realities. One could not, for example, pursue business activities under an ideal of Christian sharing in an economic system that is founded upon principles of competition. Such a practice would not only be ineffective; it would finally be dysfunctional. Troeltsch specifically rejected the presumption, advocated by some of his contemporaries, that Christian social thought consists in the application of New Testament social ideas to the institutional realities of the modern world.[16] If as Christians we are to have something to say to modern social problems, we require means of relating distinctively Christian ideas to normative understandings already resident in social processes.

B. The Necessity of Compromise in Christian Social Thought

Troeltsch's insistence upon "compromise" in Christian social thought stemmed from his recognition of the fundamental independence of basic social institutions from the central impulses of the Christian message. To address modern social problems, the Christian message must be articulated in a fashion that connects with the social realities that structure those problems. Such a connection can occur, moreover, only by way of normative ideas that already reside in social, economic, and political institutions, that is, a civilizational ethic. Thus, Christian social thought consists in the

15. The notion of "organizational principles" is taken from Jürgen Habermas. See his *Legitimation Crisis*, trans. Thomas McCarthy (Boston: Beacon Press, 1975), 7–8. See also chap. 2, 8–17.

16. See Troeltsch's critique of Nathusius's book, *Cooperation of the Church in the Solution of the Social Question*, in *Social Teaching*, 26–27.

construction of a cultural synthesis that embraces Christian ideas and a society's civilizational ethic.

A successful synthesis necessarily entails an adjustment of Christian thought to social reality. It involves compromise. Yet an effective compromise does not simply accommodate Christian convictions to ambiguous social realities; it makes possible a genuine Christian impact on those realities. At its best, it introduces something redemptive, something transforming, into social processes; in less favorable circumstances, it mitigates the damage likely to result from destructive social forces. To refuse compromise, Troeltsch believed, is to renounce all interest in a pertinent social witness.[17]

Troeltsch's contention by no means implies that any compromise whatever is morally acceptable. There are morally defensible and morally dubious compromises. It is morally absurd to peddle our souls for a mess of influence. Some systems, moreover, are so fraught with evil that we ought to resist them in every way that is compatible with our basic moral convictions. Each compromise must be assessed in light of realistic alternatives. Such complexities, however, do not alter the principal point, namely, that viable compromises are indispensable to a Christian social witness.

V. Traditions of Christian Social Thought

A. Difficulties Confronting Christian Social Ethics

To this point, Troeltsch has done little more than dramatize the difficulty of credible work in Christian social ethics. On the one hand, the earliest Christian teaching did not contain a social message. At most, it furnished resources that might be used in the development of such a message. The actual formulation of a Christian social message could only be a new creation, the fruit of the constructive imaginations of subsequent generations.

Since any social message that might arise in this fashion would surpass what was explicit in the earliest Christian teaching, we could no longer justify its claims by direct appeals to Scripture. We would have to establish its credibility on the basis of well-established traditions that enjoyed enduring authority within living communities of faith. Christian tradition is not simply the explication of ideas contained in Scripture; it develops, extends, enlarges, and transforms Scripture. It adds something novel, something unprecedented,

---

17. Ibid., 999–1004. See also Troeltsch's *Christian Thought: Its History and Application*, trans. Friedrich von Hügel, et al. (New York: Meridian Books, 1957), 123–146, where the notion of a cultural synthesis is discussed in terms of the "common spirit."

in response to new challenges. Christian social ethics centers, therefore, in the critical assessment and constructive mediation of the churches' traditions of social thought in changing social and cultural settings.

On the other hand, the basic institutions of society, perhaps especially in modern and post-modern societies, are constituted by organizational principles that are not readily amenable to distinctive Christian influences. To gain pertinence for actual social realities, any Christian social message would have to take account of normative understandings already operative in those realities. It would have to involve compromise, a synthesis of Christian ideas and the operative civilizational ethic.

A study of the social teaching of the Christian churches necessarily gives special attention, therefore, to evidence of theological interest in something like a civilizational ethic. For Troeltsch, the most promising indications of this interest were provided by theological treatments of Stoic and Aristotelian conceptions of natural law.[18] Natural law served for the classical world as the privileged vehicle of normative social thought. Its elaboration involved the analysis, interpretation, and evaluation of social and political realities in that world. These two sets of conclusions must inform our reading of Troeltsch's *Social Teaching.*

B. Traditions of "Comprehensive Historical Significance"

Surveying the major epochs of Christian social thought, Troeltsch was able to identify only two periods in church history where Christian social thought gained "comprehensive historical significance": medieval Catholicism and ascetic Protestantism.[19] Thomas Aquinas provided the definitive elaboration of the former; John Calvin set forth the foundational understandings of the latter. As Troeltsch used the term, ascetic Protestantism embraced multiple strands of reformed Protestantism, especially the "free church" traditions, and it reflected the influence of the radical Protestant sects. It reached its full practical development in Puritanism.

In variant ways Thomism and Calvinism transformed the dialectic of the primitive Christian message and its affiliated social ideas into self-conscious, critical, and comprehensive social philosophies. These philosophies, moreover, embraced normative ideas that found resonance with the principal social formations of their respective historical periods.

Apart from these two main types of Christian social philosophy,

---

18. See especially *Social Teaching*, 150–161, 259–262, 305–306.
19. See ibid., 1011. See also Troeltsch, *Christian Thought: Its History and Application*, 137, 141.

Troeltsch argued, other forms of Christian social ideas have been unable to make much impression on the "hard mass of social realities."[20] Alternative perspectives have typically sought to define the nature and limits of legitimate Christian participation in institutional arenas that are largely alien to Christian understandings.

C. Medieval Catholicism and Ascetic Protestantism

According to Troeltsch, medieval Catholicism consisted in an aristocratic social order based on family ties, craft guilds, and stable class relationships. Political authority was dispersed. The Church furnished the organizing center of society. Thomist social philosophy combined Christian convictions about the unique value of individuals and a universal fellowship of love with personal and reverential relations to those in authority. It presupposed a weak state system and relatively simple economic arrangements determined by elemental ties to the soil and a recognition of the positive value of productive labor. Its central social themes were organic unity and hierarchical order.[21] The former provided the critical principles of Christian social thought, dramatizing the solidarity of all people. The latter extended the patriarchal organization of the family to society as a whole. Its purpose was to assure order in the face of human frailties and in the presence of substantial inequalities among human beings.

Medieval Catholic social thought was essentially conservative. It presupposed the "Christian unity of civilization."[22] Drawing upon classic Aristotelian and Stoic traditions of natural law, it sought to give a coherent account of the basic institutions of society and of the roles Christians should play in those institutions. Its intent was not to "change the world," but to render the world intelligible, to display the normative standards that governed the affairs

---

20. *Social Teaching*, 1012.

21. Ibid., 280–306.

22. Ibid., 306. For Troeltsch's summary of the main features of Thomist social thought, see *Social Teaching*, 257–268.

The societal developments that gave rise to the notion of the "Christian unity of civilization," Troeltsch contended, took place during the period of the "territorial churches," extending from the sixth to the eleventh centuries. The developments of this period reached their "highest point" in the Carolingian Empire, where "an interpenetration of church and state, of the spiritual and the temporal, of the ascetic and the socio-political aspects of life" was fully realized, giving to the church of the Middle Ages a character quite different from that of the early church. See *Social Teaching*, 215, 223. Following the reassertion of papal supremacy under Gregory VII, territorialism gave way to the "ecclesiastical unity of civilization," where the unity of civilization was explicitly and practically grounded in religious, sacerdotal, sacramental, and ascetic ideas. See *Social Teaching*, 235. It was in the context of this social world that Thomas Aquinas formulated his *Summa theologicae*.

of human beings. Natural law provided the bridge between Christian ideas and existing social realities.

Medieval Catholic social thought did not take on a critical cast until it began to confront modern phenomena such as emergent capitalism, the class struggle, the formation of powerful nation-states, the development of democratic institutions, the growth of the empirical sciences, and the influence of Enlightenment rationalism. Over against these modern constructions, Catholic teaching called for a conscious and systematic return to "natural principles." Troeltsch read *Rerum Novarum,* the landmark encyclical of Leo XIII, in these terms, though he credited Leo with recognizing the new social situation of Catholic workers.[23]

As a social philosophy, Calvinism was from its beginnings self-consciously world-transforming. Originating in the thriving town culture of sixteenth- and seventeenth-century Europe, it sought, under the leadership of God's elect, to create a Holy Commonwealth where all citizens would be subject to the binding authority of God's sovereign will as revealed in Scripture. In formulating his social thought, Calvin did not look first to New Testament materials. He turned rather to the study of Pentateuchal laws and ordinances, which he interpreted with a sophisticated awareness of their social and historical contexts. These codes provided authoritative resources for the generation of a new body of civil law applicable to the circumstances of sixteenth-century Geneva. By virtue of their original links to the concrete social realities of ancient Israel, the Pentateuchal codes could instruct the faithful in their efforts to articulate God's will for the governance of free European cities. Natural law traditions informed these efforts, though not in the explicit, systematic manner characteristic of Thomism.[24]

Ascetic Protestantism, Troeltsch observed, eventually embraced utilitarianism and rationalism, especially their accent on democracy, liberalism, and individualism. It neutralized somewhat the morally dangerous tendencies in these ideas by stressing the responsibility of the individual for the commonweal: the duty to love the neighbor and to promote the common good. With its taboos on luxury and on indulgence in fleshly pleasures, and with its

---

23. *Social Teaching,* 304, nl44a.

24. Ibid., 621–623. In Troeltsch's reading, it was the Calvinist doctrine of election that provided the driving energy for world-transforming activism. For Calvinists, the world was, in effect, reduced to a mere "means" for glorifying God.

Troeltsch contrasts primitive Calvinism and Neo-Calvinism. The latter refers principally to Puritanism. It alone fully embodied what Troeltsch called "ascetic Protestantism." For a summary of the social philosophy of primitive Calvinism, see *Social Teaching,* 652–655. Troeltsch gives special attention to the "democratic tendencies" in Calvinism (*Social Teaching,* 628–630), and to the relation of Calvinism to capitalism (*Social Teaching,* 644–650).

emphasis on the heroic service of Christ all over the world, it also subjected to the sovereign rule of God the notions it embraced. Thus, ascetic Protestantism found ways to incorporate the major trends of early modernity.[25]

D. The Decline of Christian Social Thought

Despite their historic importance, Troeltsch believed, the two major types of Christian social thought were largely spent by the first decade of the twentieth century. Neither was likely to exercise influence comparable to that which it enjoyed in its period of ascendancy. Troeltsch based his judgment in part on the fact that European patterns of religious establishment were effectively coming to an end. In neither Roman Catholic nor Protestant territories was the church still able to function as the paramount social institution, and, hence, as the privileged locus of normative moral teaching.

Troeltsch also doubted, however, that either of these two great traditions of Christian social thought could authentically embrace the dominant social forces of the modern world. He had in mind a robust nationalism ideologically linked to the formation of large, bureaucratic states, and an energetic capitalism governed by free market exchange and marked by the provocation of class struggle.

In response to these new forces, Troeltsch contended, Roman Catholic teaching increasingly turned inward to deal with problems of ecclesiastical order. Despite the attention devoted to the plight of industrial labor by *Rerum Novarum,* its social witness provided no sanction for class struggle—though motifs of struggle were not excluded altogether. On the basis of its organic conception of "natural" social relations, its vision of the social good involved the transcendence of class conflict. The investment in organicism likewise inhibited any Catholic disposition to embrace the capitalist celebration of free-market competition. Troeltsch could have made similar observations about the role that hierarchical conceptions of institutional order played in shaping Roman Catholic responses to democratic institutions and bureaucratic state systems. Over against the class struggle, free-market competition, the formation of democratic institutions, and the emergence of large bureaucratic states, Catholic social thought continued to cling to classic organic and hierarchical notions.[26] Troeltsch's claim was that neither of these notions was well-suited to the realities of the modern world.

25. Ibid., 688–691.
26. Ibid., 306–311. See also 1010–1013. In my judgment, Troeltsch's general characterization of Roman Catholic social teaching continues to hold for all of the great social encyclicals, and also for the pastoral letters of American Catholic bishops. On this point, see in particular David Hollenbach's discus-

Following Max Weber's analysis, Troeltsch believed that ascetic Protestantism was considerably more compatible with modern social forces, especially elemental democratic and capitalist development.[27] At the same time, he believed that ascetic Protestantism was itself undergoing transformation into what he termed mystical types of piety and religious association. Public and institutional forms of religious devotion were giving way to highly individualized, privatized patterns of faith existence. As I have noted, the latter allow room only for a weak and unstable organizational structure, that is, the voluntary association of like-minded individuals.[28]

Troeltsch did see in the aggressive sects of the Protestant Reformation understandings that could under certain circumstances become features in a larger movement of social renewal. He interpreted the Christian socialism of his time as one such development. In his assessment, however, Christian socialism remained secondary in significance to the "great socialist movement" itself. At best, it had only been able to interpret, appropriate, and qualify the latter. Christianity does not breed social revolution, Troeltsch asserted.[29]

Troeltsch's claim is a subtle one. He is fully aware of the active role of ascetic Protestantism in at least two revolutions, the seventeenth-century Puritan revolution in Great Britain, and the eighteenth-century American revolution. His argument rests upon his prior assessment of the nature of the primitive Christian message in relation to the subsequent European realization of the "ecclesiastical unity of civilization."

On the one hand, the primitive Christian message did not give rise to radical movements for social change. When the earliest Christians faced oppressive social conditions, their leaders counseled patient waiting and faithful enduring, leaving to God actions that would establish God's Kingdom. On the other hand, once Christianity had adjusted itself to the world in the "ecclesiastical unity of civilization," a commitment to radical world transformation could be introduced into Christianity only from the outside, principally through the pressure of intolerable social conditions.

Even more important, thought capable of informing radical commitments to social reform could only arise from modern social philosophies. These

sion of *Laborem exercens* and *Octogesima adveniens*, and also his treatment of *Economic Justice for All: Pastoral Letter on Catholic Social Teaching and the U.S. Economy,* in *Justice, Peace, and Human Rights: American Catholic Social Ethics in a Pluralistic World* (New York: Crossroad, 1988), especially 18–25, 79–83, 95–98.

27. The reference is to Max Weber, *The Protestant Ethic and the Spirit of Capitalism* (New York: Charles Scribner's Sons, 1958). See n. 24 above.

28. *Social Teaching,* 381. See also 377–378, 991–992, and 1008–1010.

29. Ibid., 818.

latter philosophies took shape through critical reflection on social conditions and on the dynamics of social movements striving to change those conditions. Just as modern democratic ideas infused both Puritan and American revolutions, especially the latter, so Marxist thought was central to socialist activities in the late nineteenth and early twentieth centuries. These modern social philosophies shared an interest in the social sciences and confidence in technological conceptions of progress.

On the basis of this multi-faceted analysis, Troeltsch concluded that Christian socialism could not be considered an original outgrowth of the Gospel itself. It was rather a response and an adaptation to European socialist movements. Troeltsch would doubtless have interpreted the more recent liberation theologies in a similar fashion: Christian accompaniments and adaptations to liberation struggles.[30]

Troeltsch did acknowledge that Christian socialism could appeal to the Gospel as a warrant for its activities. It could do so, however, only within "free voluntary communities," that is, as a radical, sectarian movement. Socialistic churches, he concluded, are "nonsense."[31]

The results of Troeltsch's investigations are sobering: the main types of Christian social thought, despite their great and enduring achievements, no longer have the capacity to play a formative role in European social evolution. In the face of the tasks they now confront, they have become largely powerless. Indeed, Troeltsch adds, all Christian social involvements are now in a problematic condition. If the churches are to recover a substantive social witness, he suggested, they must learn to think thoughts that they have never thought before.[32]

---

30. See ibid., 804–805, 817–818. Troeltsch's claims, it should be emphasized, do not imply that Christians should under no circumstances become participants either in the European class struggle or in contemporary liberation struggles. His point is rather that Christian socialism did not amount to a "comprehensive Christian social philosophy of world historical importance" in the same sense as medieval Catholicism and ascetic Protestantism. Its role was to furnish warrants for Christian participation in a social movement determined by principles that were not only independent of the Christian message but also fundamentally alien to it.

To make the same point in Troeltsch's technical categories: Christian socialism did not yet constitute an effective compromise with socialist thought. Indeed, Troeltsch did not appear to believe that such a compromise was even possible given the Gospel's predisposition to repudiate the "struggle for existence." At best, therefore, Christian thought could only "accompany" the socialist movement or "adapt itself" to that movement, on the analogy of earlier Christian adaptations to imperial Rome. Such accompaniments and adaptations themselves attest to the fact that Christian social thought of world-historical importance may have ceased to be a realistic possibility. Thus, any Christian social witness that might now be offered would probably have to be described in similar terms!

31. Ibid., 805.

32. Ibid., 1012.

IV. Christian Social Thought in the American Context

A. The Informal Protestant Establishment

Troeltsch's negative assessment of the prospects of Christian social teaching was, at the time of his writing, premature with regard to the American churches. Throughout the greater part of the twentieth century, the American churches have displayed considerable vigor, and they have exercised no small amount of influence in the public life of the nation. However, his gloomy prognosis has now begun to appear germane to the American setting.

The major traditions of social teaching highlighted by Troeltsch—medieval Catholicism and ascetic Protestantism—have also furnished two of the preeminent forms of Christian public witness in the United States. In the American setting, the order of historical precedence of these traditions has been reversed. It was ascetic Protestantism that played the formative role in the initial development of basic American institutions, while Roman Catholic social teaching did not begin to win a place for itself until the early decades of the twentieth century.

From early in the nineteenth century, moreover, these two traditions had to make their way in a legal framework of disestablishment. Robert Handy argues that Protestant groups readily accepted First Amendment strictures on religious establishment because of the persistence of an informal Protestant establishment.[33] Indeed, for evangelical Protestants an informal establishment was actually the more congenial arrangement. It was in full accord with their belief that the church is a gathered community of believers. One enters the church only by publicly confessing Jesus Christ as Savior and Lord. As a matter of principle, such a church could never be formally established. Through waves of revivals, evangelical Protestants hoped to win the nation and eventually the world for Christ. They expected that the converted would manifest the new birth in their social existence. No other social witness was needed.

During the informal Protestant establishment, the "denomination type" replaced the "church type" as the church's paramount organizational form. The denomination delineated a limited number of acceptable variants on a shared set of religious convictions and practices, in this case, those broadly termed Protestant.[34] Though Protestant groups were frequently involved in

33. Robert Handy, *A Christian America: Protestant Hopes and Historical Realities*, 2d ed., revised and enlarged (New York: Oxford University Press, 1984), 20, 22.
34. See ibid., 22, 27. In a society that was pervasively Protestant, the denomination was a functional equivalent of the "church type." In a genuinely pluralistic society, it has more affinities with the "mystical

doctrinal disputes, they also acknowledged their participation in a common family of belief and practice. No one denomination had preeminent standing; all had relative legitimacy. Constitutional constraints protected these contrasting values.

The "denomination" did not, as we sometimes suppose, encompass religious pluralism. Roman Catholicism, for example, did not constitute an acceptable variant within the Protestant establishment. It was perceived to be a betrayal of the Gospel, and, as such, a threat both to American piety and to widely shared American values.[35] For that matter, Roman Catholics also did not understand themselves as one Christian denomination alongside the many Protestant denominations. They were loyal to the one holy catholic and apostolic church in a society under the dominion of Protestant errors.

In a similar fashion, other religious groups also fell outside the acceptable range of Protestant variation. Mormonism is a noteworthy instance. Ironically, Jews were more likely to be considered an acceptable minority, in large measure because of their small numbers. Protestant leaders celebrated the fact that Jews had found asylum in a free America, while also viewing them as an occasion for an evangelistic mission.[36] Non-Protestant groups did enjoy Constitutional protection, but the formal guarantees they received were significantly qualified by the pervasive presence of Protestant understandings in American social institutions.

B. Evangelical Protestant Social Teaching

Within the context of the informal Protestant establishment, evangelical Protestantism generated a new model of Christian social thought. Strong elements of ascetic Protestantism persisted, especially conceptions of Christian discipline leading to holiness of life. The evangelical social vision, however, was not Holy Commonwealth, but Christian America.[37] This vision was both less and more than that offered by ascetic Protestantism. It was more in that it sought the conversion of all, not simply God's elect. For evangelicals, there were no reprobates, only sinners who had not yet repented. It was less in that

---

type" of social organization, where the churches are private associations of like-minded individuals. In the latter case, the crucial question is whether the churches can any longer generate and sustain an effective social witness, especially one that authentically emerges out of their understandings of their distinctive mission. It may be well, however, to think of the "denomination" as a distinct type in its own right, one that has a unique way of processing individualistic and universalistic tendencies in the Christian message.

35. Ibid., 51–52.

36. See ibid., 52.

37. See ibid., chap. 2, "A Complete Christian Commonwealth," 24–37.

it did not explicitly entail Christian oversight of governmental offices as a means of enforcing God's sovereign will in society. There was, Handy notes, a bias toward voluntarism in evangelical Protestantism.[38] This bias derived from the evangelical conviction that conversion requires not only divine grace, but also the willing consent of the converted. With regard to voluntarism, evangelical Protestants shared common ground with "free church" Calvinists.

When evangelical Protestants first entered the legislative arena, they were chiefly interested in establishing public conditions that would facilitate the evangelical revival, such things as the protection of the Christian sabbath, constraints on public vice, and the promotion of public schools. Under the tutelage of evangelical teachers, public schools functioned as Protestant schools, actively nurturing Protestant piety. Apart from interests such as these, evangelical Protestants expected Christian influences to permeate the social order through the voluntary activities of the converted.[39] The political program of the religious new right is largely continuous with the substance of nineteenth-century evangelical Protestant convictions.[40]

The Social Gospel was more a fruit of the evangelical vision of Christian America than of the Puritan vision of Holy Commonwealth. In seeking to Christianize the social order, spokespersons for the Social Gospel were not merely seeking to instruct the elect while constraining the reprobate. They were seeking the total transformation of life for all people. What was new was the conviction that the Gospel embraces social and institutional change as well as personal conversion, and that the former is not automatically accomplished through the latter. By its critical attention to social and institutional realities, the Social Gospel transformed the evangelical Protestant legacy into a genuine social philosophy "of comprehensive historical significance." This philosophy not only offered a credible account of the social implications of the Gospel. It also incorporated into its normative understandings notions that were resident in basic social and political institutions.

The Social Gospel readily claimed as its own the principles of liberal

38. Ibid., 37–47.

39. Ibid., 74–81, 87–90.

40. See Mark A. Noll, Nathan O. Hatch, and George M. Marsden, eds., *The Search for Christian America* (Westchester, IL: Crossway Books, 1983); and Robert C. Liebman and Robert Wuthnow, eds., *The New Christian Right: Mobilization and Legitimation* (New York: Aldine Publishing Co., 1983). Other relevant studies include Jon Butler, *Awash in a Sea of Faith: Christianizing the American People* (Cambridge, MA: Harvard University Press, 1990), and especially, Mark A. Noll, ed., *Religion and American Politics: From the Colonial Period to the 1980s* (New York: Oxford University Press, 1990). See also my paper "Renewing Ecumenical Protestant Social Thought," in Douglas Knight and Peter Paris, eds., *Justice and the Holy* (Atlanta: Scholars Press, 1989), 401. [Reprinted as chapter 5 in this volume.]

democracy that undergirded American political institutions. It struggled, though with less clarity and with still less agreement, to come to terms with the realities of an emerging industrial economy. Some interpreters sought initially to displace capitalism with democratic socialism. Others promoted a system of consumer cooperatives alongside private enterprises. Eventually, these radical responses yielded to a complex array of more pragmatic strategies, usually involving some form of governmental intervention in the economy. These latter strategies sought to constrain the excesses of capitalism and to compensate for its failures while also protecting the essential conditions for the realization of its productive potential.[41] In respect to both democratic and capitalist institutions, the Social Gospel comprised a synthesis of Christian convictions and American civilizational values.

The Social Gospel gained organizational expression in a great variety of voluntary associations, but preeminently in newly founded ecumenical bodies, that is, the Federal Council of Churches, which later became the National Council of Churches, and the World Council of Churches. Though these ecumenical bodies have had a wide range of interests, it is not inappropriate to associate them with an ecumenical Protestant social witness, one that combined ascetic Protestant and evangelical Protestant traditions in an affirmation of the Social Gospel. Thus, the Social Gospel became the social philosophy of ecumenical Protestantism.

The independent African-American churches offered an important counterpart to European-American versions of evangelical Protestantism. Insofar as those churches constituted the institutional center of African-American communities, they functioned as a practical religious establishment. They were key sources of energy for organized struggles to abolish slavery and, subsequently, to end legal segregation. They also promoted the social and cultural advancement of African-American peoples. The African-American Christian traditions explicitly embodied the cultural synthesis of which Troeltsch spoke, combining Christian proclamations of the fatherhood of God and the "brotherhood" of all people with advocacy for American traditions of freedom.[42]

41. See in particular Walter Rauschenbusch's classic, *Christianizing the Social Order* (New York: Macmillan, 1913). On the relation of the Social Gospel to evangelical Protestantism, see Donald W. Dayton, *Discovering an Evangelical Heritage* (New York: Harper & Row, 1984).

42. Peter Paris refers to these notions as the "prophetic principle" of the Black Christian tradition. See *The Social Teaching of the Black Churches* (Philadelphia: Fortress Press, 1985), 10–13. Though C. Eric Lincoln and Lawrence H. Mamiya conclude their recently published study with the judgment that the African-American churches remain, on the whole, healthy and vibrant institutions, they do note signs of difficulty in these churches that could forecast future decline for them as well. See *The Black Church in the African American Experience* (Durham, NC: Duke University Press, 1990), 382–398.

In Handy's reading, the informal Protestant establishment largely collapsed following the First World War.[43] This "second dis-establishment" was caused by many factors, not least of which were the fundamentalist-modernist controversies that divided both evangelical and reformed Protestants into conservative and liberal wings. To complicate matters further, the latter divisions did not necessarily result in new congregations or denominations. They displayed ideological conflicts internal to existing churches and denominations.

Of no less importance, however, were the waves of new immigrants who dramatically increased the number of Roman Catholics and Jews in the population. The demographic shift meant that there would be a new kind of resistance to the evangelical project of Christianizing America, one borne not by unbelief but by positive convictions of an alternative sort. The new immigrant groups, moreover, were prominent in the worker movement with which Protestant advocates of the Social Gospel had allied themselves. Finally, as the worker movement confronted the effective opposition of industrial leaders and their political allies, the zeal and optimism of the Social Gospel had to be tempered by a new sense of "realism," bringing into sharper relief the complexity and ambiguity of social and political involvements in modern industrial and urban societies.[44]

In no small measure, it was the collapse of the informal Protestant establishment that made room for the development of indigenous American appropriations of Roman Catholic social teaching. This development presupposed credible reformulations of classic Catholic traditions in relation to the principles of liberal democracy and the circumstances of religious pluralism.[45] The rise of indigenous Catholic social thought was also facilitated by the formal teaching authority of the bishops. When American Catholic bishops have exercised their teaching office in discriminating ways, they have often been more effective than Protestant leaders in setting forth a cogent Christian social vision.

---

43. Handy, *A Christian America*, 174–185.

44. In my view, Reinhold Niebuhr did not so much invent "Christian realism" as introduce it afresh into ecumenical Protestant discourse. He accomplished this task by drawing upon the legacy of Augustine and early catholic Christianity, on the one hand, and Martin Luther and the Reformation in Germany, on the other. The social situation of the American churches made them receptive to this realist voice.

45. John A. Ryan did the pioneering work in the formulation of an indigenous American appropriation of Roman Catholic social thought. A prolific author, Ryan's books include *A Living Wage: Its Ethical and Political Aspects* (New York: Macmillan, 1906); *Distributive Justice: The Right and Wrong of Our Present Distribution of Wealth* (New York: Macmillan, 1916); *Social Reconstruction* (New York: Macmillan, 1920); *The Catholic Church and the Citizen* (New York: Macmillan, 1928). With Francis J. Boland, S.J., he was co-author of *Catholic Principles of Politics* (New York: Macmillan, 1940). His autobiography is

C. Conflict and Division within a Pluralistic Society

In contemporary America, there are multiple religious constituencies with distinctive socio-political traditions. Many of these groups have an interest in a public role, most notably, ecumenical Protestants, evangelical Protestants, African-American Protestants, and Roman Catholics. To these historically prominent participants in American public life one must at least add the major Jewish communities, churches in the Orthodox traditions, classic Reformation churches that have previously had only a limited role in the formation of ecumenical Protestant social teaching, and Pentecostal and Holiness churches.

In this pluralistic context, the term "denomination" takes on a new meaning. It no longer refers to mutually recognized and tolerated differences within a broad Protestant establishment. It now tends to refer to religious bodies that are quite diverse on fundamental matters, so that the Roman Catholic Church or the Greek Orthodox Church or even the principal Jewish bodies become "denominations" of a sort. They exist side by side as multiple expressions of organized religious life, and they interact to some degree at the boundaries, especially on public matters. None of these groups has preeminent standing within the society; all enjoy Constitutional protection for the "free exercise of religion" so long as they do not encroach upon the rights of others with different persuasions.

The picture is further complicated by the fact that these religious bodies disagree, both internally and among themselves, on many public issues. The internal disagreements suggest that particular church bodies no longer have coherent socio-political perspectives. In many instances, congregations and denominations do not so much nurture a shared view of the world as reflect within their membership the diversity of views already found in the society. The older traditions have broken down as resources for a social witness, and the "mystical type" of association has gained ground, weakening denominational discipline.

---

entitled *Social Doctrine in Action: A Personal History* (New York: Harper and Brothers, 1941). In more recent decades, John Courtney Murray has provided basic studies of the relation of Roman Catholicism to American democratic principles. He published a collection of seminal essays under the title, *We Hold These Truths: Catholic Reflections on the American Proposition* (New York: Sheed and Ward, 1960). See also his *The Problem of Religious Freedom* (Westminster, MD: Newman Press, 1965). Finally, see Murray's discussion of the declaration on religious freedom at Vatican II, entitled, "The Declaration on Religious Freedom," in *Vatican II: An Interfaith Appraisal*, ed. John E. Miller (Notre Dame, IN: University of Notre Dame Press, 1966).

For a broad historical treatment, see Charles E. Curran, *American Catholic Social Ethics: Twentieth-Century Approaches* (Notre Dame, IN: University of Notre Dame Press, 1982).

By virtue of its voluntarist sensibilities, evangelical Protestantism actually fostered mystical forms of ecclesial organization. The practical import of voluntarism is, however, profoundly affected by the larger social and cultural context. Voluntary associations could have considerable vitality and public effectiveness in the context of an overarching Protestant establishment. They are more likely to be organizationally weak and publicly ineffective in a secular, religiously plural society, especially where there are few cultural or institutional supports for their basic beliefs and practices.

In a pluralist context, commitment to religious associations tends to become provisional and restricted. Individuals support an association only to the degree that they find its policies and practices congenial. Otherwise, they feel free to limit their support or perhaps to withdraw from participation altogether. When the churches are reduced to associations of this sort, they have considerable difficulty sustaining the accountabilities that are necessary for an effective social witness. Recognizing these realities, policy makers cease to believe that the public pronouncements of church leaders any longer represent the views of their constituents.[46]

Within ecumenical Protestantism in particular, the question of legitimate authority has become acute. Who has the right to define the churches' witness and under what circumstances? By what process shall the churches arrive at a shared socio-political vision? What shall be the nature of that vision? Must it be restricted to general principles of moral judgment? Can it include particular recommendations on specific policy matters? If the latter, what specialized knowledge of a nontheological sort is required? In recent years, these matters have been subject to considerable debate.[47]

Disagreements between religious bodies have further added to the difficulties of a Christian public witness. Rather than enriching public discourse about the common good, the churches' attempts to introduce their social teaching into the public arena have become a divisive force in the American body politic. In response, many would remove religious bodies from any involvement in public life, except perhaps where those bodies have a direct stake in a policy matter. In the latter instances, churches and denominations would function not as the conscience of society, but as one more special interest group,

---

46. On the breakdown of denominations, see especially Robert Wuthnow, *The Restructuring of American Religion: Society and Faith Since World War II* (Princeton: Princeton University Press, 1988).

47. Paul Ramsey, *Who Speaks for the Church: A Critique of the 1966 Geneva Conference on Church and Society* (Nashville: Abingdon Press, 1967), was the first to raise these questions in a sustained way. Questions about authority have now become central to reflections on the social teaching of the churches. See in this connection Timothy Sedgwick and Philip Turner, eds., *The Crisis of Moral Teaching in the Episcopal Church* (Harrisburg, PA: Morehouse Barlow, 1992).

like the National Rifle Association. Policy makers understand the churches when they act as special interests. They readily take their needs into account in efforts to balance, coordinate, and perhaps mobilize multiple special interests. Such is the stuff of contemporary politics. Policy makers are apt to find intrusive any actions by religious bodies to promote a wider public good on the basis of fundamental religious and moral beliefs.

Troeltsch's earlier assessment has become more compelling: the major traditions of Christian social thought appear to have lost their capacity to shape modern social forces. If a Christian witness is to be renewed in the American setting, thoughts may have to be thought that have never been thought before.

V. Muddling Through: Rethinking the Churches' Public Vocation

In the secular, pluralistic environment of the present, Christians will undoubtedly have to surrender their earlier aspirations after comprehensive social philosophies of world-historical importance. Such a goal has not only become unrealistic; it may even have become illegitimate since it would entail the practical restoration of a religious establishment. In theological terms, it would amount to a refusal to honor the God-ordained orders of life that make social existence possible in a fallen world.

There is, however, middle ground between church-type social hegemony and mystical-type abdication of public responsibility. That middle ground consists of substantive Christian contributions to a multi-faceted, multicultural, ecumenical, and interfaith discourse on the common good, one that both protects the free exercise of religion and also seeks publicly shared grounds for addressing the great social questions of the day. Where such shared grounds cannot be uncovered, there must be a readiness to experiment with partial, even makeshift measures, provided they can mitigate social suffering and also protect future opportunities for more satisfactory solutions. Churches can have something to say to modern social problems without presuming to say everything and certainly without claiming to offer the final word.

A. Nurturing Ecclesial Bonds

How might the churches undertake even this relatively modest task? Before the churches can accomplish anything that is socially significant, they will have to find ways of resisting the mystical tendencies, noted by Troeltsch, that threaten the viability of their organizational expressions. To be the church, it is not enough to remain simply a voluntary association of like-minded individuals. The church is a community of persons bound to Jesus Christ and to one another in covenant faithfulness. As such, the church endures over time and takes form in multiple social and cultural settings. On the basis of a fresh engagement with the substance of the Christian Gospel, the churches must learn again how to nurture and strengthen the communal bonds that characterize living communities of faith. Such bonds are essential to the churches' being.[48] They sustain vital communities, which alone have the power to shape human lives and mold human perceptions; they foster the discernment necessary to a critical assessment of the churches' traditions of social thought in their bearing on new social realities.[49]

This ecclesial emphasis cannot be limited to a purely congregational focus, especially one that is isolated from the churches' global manifestations. By themselves, local congregations can become quite provincial in outlook. They tend toward a social and cultural homogeneity that belies the church's inherent inclusiveness. Consequently, congregations have to recover an appreciation for the necessity of denominational and ecumenical connections. They have to rebuild their loyalties to the churches' more complex organizational expressions. Where such loyalties are present, local congregations have access to the church's racial and cultural diversity. They become involved in mission to "all sorts and conditions" of human beings. Denominational and ecumenical loyalties can be renewed, however, only insofar as the churches' leaders themselves embody a new sense of accountability for their own activities to concrete worshipping communities.

B. Critically Reconstructing Traditions of Social Teaching

In the context of ecclesial interactions, the churches must provide substantial settings for reflection on what might be the distinctive contributions of the Christian churches to the great social questions of the day. This reflection will be guided by the formative traditions of the various churches. Indeed, it proceeds by the assessment and critical mediation of those traditions in their bearing on the contemporary world. While we may be obliged to "think thoughts that have never been thought before," these new thoughts will consist chiefly in the critical reconstruction of received traditions.

Thus, Roman Catholic social thought will serve best by continuing to

---

48. Troeltsch underscored this point as well. See *Social Teaching*, 1006–1007.

49. I argued this point initially in my presidential address to the Society of Christian Ethics, "The Ecclesial Context of Christian Ethics," *The Annual of the Society of Christian Ethics,* 1984. [Reprinted as an appendix to this volume.] See also "Renewing Ecumenical Protestant Social Teaching," in *Justice and the Holy,* 398–399. [Reprinted as chapter 5 in this volume.]

explicate organic visions of society, tempered by realistic concerns for viable structures of social order. Ecumenical Protestants will serve best by reclaiming ascetic Protestant interests in the well-ordered society, combined with Social Gospel commitments to the transformation of societal institutions in order to promote justice in the world. Above all, ecumenical Protestants need to incorporate the historic resistance of the African-American churches to racism and their determination to foster the practical development of all peoples. Similarly, ecumenical Protestants must move forward with feminist insistence upon the full equality of women in church and society. Finally, in charting a separate role for themselves, evangelical Protestants will do well to reclaim historic Protestant concerns for family values, public morals, and an appropriate loyalty to the nation, provided they also renounce any ideological use of these themes to cover exploitative and oppressive social practices.

These ecclesial traditions are all ambiguous, even flawed. They all require continual criticism and reconstruction. Yet they all contain genuine insight into the nature of the good society. Indeed, the flaws that mar the various traditions persist primarily because of their links to what is sound and good. Critique is inescapably controversial, perhaps one-sided, even prone to excesses, because it must expose the negative underside of traditions that enjoy normative authority. Nonetheless, a discerning critique remains an essential part of the churches' public discourse. The goal of the discourse is the further development of the received traditions in relation to contemporary realities. The principal question becomes: how might traditions of Christian social thought be reconstructed so that they can contribute to a public discourse about the common good within a secular, religiously plural body politic?

At its best, the critical mediation of normative traditions manifests the individualism-universalism dialectic that Troeltsch discerned in the primitive Christian Gospel. Regard for the continuity of tradition captures the Gospel's universalist interest in provisional order and stability; commitment to the criticism and reconstruction of tradition reinstates the individualist challenge to prevailing patterns of order for the sake of God's coming realm. In organizational terms, church-type structures motivate an interest in consensual agreements or in compromises that preserve institutional stability in the face of chronic conflict. The official pronouncements of churches, denominations, and ecumenical associations are characteristically constrained by this church-type interest. In contrast, activist caucuses are sectarian in structure, aggressively promoting the more radical understandings of Christian fidelity in the face of ecclesiastical caution. In many instances, Christian churches and denominations have found ways to institutionalize the activities of special-interest caucuses in order to incorporate their critical contributions into normal ecclesiastical deliberations. In so doing, they recognize the church-sect contrast as a crucial feature of the church's quest for fidelity and effectiveness.

The churches do not have to have ready access to policy makers in order to engage in a public discourse. They only require a readiness to create public settings where Christians can think together about the issues of the day. No particular church or denomination can attend to all matters of importance, but it would be possible for various churches to focus selectively on particular sets of problems that are especially urgent. Where such inquiries are properly pursued, they make use of the specialized knowledge of well-informed lay persons who are able to grasp and interpret the technical aspects of policy issues.[50]

When public discourse within the churches moves toward policy recommendations, it will invariably become controversial. No analysis of difficult social issues proceeds without confronting the ideological disputes that revolve around those issues. Conflicting ideologies represent divergent ways of coping with particular problems, even when their underlying motivation is denial or avoidance. Christians concerned with the churches' social teaching have to learn, therefore, to analyze and assess the prevailing ideologies and the underlying interests that furnish their driving energy. Normative traditions of Christian social thought, critically interpreted, provide the measure for evaluating the various ideologies.

C. Ecumenical and Interfaith Conversations

If Christian churches are to encourage public discourse about the common good in a secular, religiously plural society, they have no choice but to pursue that discourse, at least in part, in ecumenical and interfaith contexts. The underlying presumption in any advocacy of a Christian public witness is that

---

50. As examples, see the "Pastoral Letter," United Methodist Council of Bishops, *In Defense of Creation: The Nuclear Crisis and a Just Peace* (Nashville: The Graded Press, 1986); The Commission for Church and Society of the Evangelical Lutheran Church of America, *Abortion: A Call to Deliberate* (Chicago, 1990); and The 203rd General Assembly Response to the Report of the Special Committee on Human Sexuality, *Presbyterians and Human Sexuality* (Louisville: Office of the General Assembly, Presbyterian Church [U.S.A.], 1991). The Presbyterian document contains majority and minority reports of the "Special Committee." Both were rejected by the General Assembly, but commended for study by the churches. The ELCA document was adopted by the denomination's General Assembly. A preparatory document, also produced by the Commission for Church and Society, *The Church in Society: Toward a Lutheran Perspective* (Chicago, 1989), described the deliberative process needed in treatments of controversial public issues.

religious communities have a right to participate in public discourse about the common good, even within a Constitutional framework that proscribes religious establishment. The First Amendment is not about the separation of church and state, but about the free exercise of religion and the prohibition of religious establishment. If Christian churches are to honor this framework, they cannot simply press their own agenda while dismissing, ignoring, or trivializing different views expressed by other religious bodies. Church leaders have a responsibility to deepen public understanding of the elemental sources of conflict within and among various religious bodies. They must equip themselves to display what is at stake, morally and religiously, in the disputes that seriously divide religious communities.

If church leaders are to fulfill these responsibilities, they require skills in constructing bases for a common life in a diverse, even fragmented, society despite the persistence of serious disagreements. Various participants in a public discourse have to be able to describe fairly what they disagree about and why. They have to become more inventive in proposing ways of living and working together even when they cannot resolve their differences. In this undertaking, biblical admonitions to patience and forbearance play no small role.

Efforts to clarify and mitigate, perhaps even resolve, significant conflicts does not imply that individuals should take their own convictions lightly. Each must steadfastly defend what he or she thinks to be true, right, and good, even to the point of declaring forthrightly that contrary views are false or morally indefensible. The most earnest attempts to achieve mutual understanding sometimes reach an impasse. Since all human understanding is finite, relative, ambiguous, even flawed, there remains an obligation to continue striving for deeper understanding of the views of those who see and think differently. Christians concerned with a social witness have a responsibility to display publicly the meaning and significance of persisting religious disagreements, for the sake of a more civil and fruitful public discourse. In ecumenical and interfaith exchanges, particular ecclesial communities gain resources to correct and supplement their own traditions, enhancing their fidelity to the Gospel from which they draw their sustenance.

D. Entering the Public Discourse

In their internal conversations, the churches properly draw upon the fullness of Christian tradition in its promise for the common life of all. In their ecumenical and interfaith discourse, particular ecclesial communities also learn to attend receptively to similarly rich traditions borne by other religious bodies. They seek areas of congruence while also striving to identify irresolvable differences. They seize opportunities to correct and supplement their own taken-for-granted understandings.

However, when Christians attempt to reconstruct their traditions in their bearing on the resolution of difficult social problems in a secular, religiously plural society, they have to recast insights derived from their traditions in forms appropriate to the society's public life. Just as Christian discourse had to become, first, ecumenical discourse among interpreters of diverse ecclesial traditions, and, then, religious discourse within an interfaith context, so finally it must become civil discourse within an essentially secular body politic. To speak to contemporary public issues, the churches must learn to articulate the salient features of their own distinctive witness in relation to values broadly shared within the body politic. Here we return once again to Troeltsch's conception of a "civilizational ethic."

Christian social ethics itself involves the critical scrutiny of ideas such as the American civil religion or an American public ethics. It also requires attentiveness to an "otherness" within the complex, multi-faceted American story that disturbs the dominion of more classic concepts of what it means to be American. This "otherness" is borne principally by those who have been left out, marginalized, or exploited in the course of American history, especially Native Americans, African-Americans, immigrant communities from Eastern and Southern Europe, and more recently, from Asia, Latin America, Africa, and the Middle East. A form of "otherness" has been borne by women generally, who at best have experienced only sporadic and uneven gains in the public life of the nation. There are now new levels of awareness about the "otherness" experienced by persons with gay and lesbian sexual orientations. A sense of "otherness" is one of the sources of radical criticism within American society. Its organizational expressions are often analogous in form to sectarian structures within Christianity. In regard to both the reigning civilizational ethic and the patterns of otherness that challenge it, the public witness of the churches includes an interest in advancing the moral substance of civil discourse within a secular, religiously plural society.[51]

In formulating their social witness, we could say that Christians have to become multi-lingual: they have to speak the language of their own traditions, the languages of more or less parallel ecclesial traditions, the languages of diverse non-Christian religious bodies, and the language of civil society. I would even contend that the churches must forego the public advocacy of notions distinctive to their own traditions where those notions are

51. The reference to "otherness" is inspired by Charles Long's plenary address at the opening session of the Society of Christian Ethics in Philadelphia, PA, January, 1992.

fundamentally incompatible with a public ethic. To paraphrase St. Paul, the mandate is: subject yourselves to the shared normative framework that orders the society in which you find yourselves, for such frameworks are of God. I suspect that we can legitimately set aside such a mandate only in a *status confessionis* where we judge the society's normative framework to be functionally idolatrous. In most cases, the reigning civilizational ethic offers the only promising basis for the promotion of common grounds of understanding.

At this point, Christian social ethics involves various forms of "compromise" with the reigning civilizational ethic. In the American context, as I have noted, the civilizational ethic consists chiefly in principles of liberal democracy and the traditions of human and civil liberties upon which they are founded. It also embraces capitalist values, especially notions of disciplined work, prudent judgment, and individual initiative and enterprise. These latter notions have generally been qualified in Christian social thought by an emphasis on the democratic regulation of economic activities in the interest of societal well-being.[52]

Despite its importance, the reigning civilizational ethic is by no means sacrosanct. It must continually be subjected to criticism in light of actual social and political realities. Christian perspectives properly inform such criticism. Yet the society's civilizational ethic remains the most promising starting point for principles and values capable of sustaining a public discourse within a pluralistic society. Christians bear a significant share of responsibility for sustaining the conditions for such a discourse in the interest of the common good. They can properly advocate their own distinctive contribution to the common good when they also honor the conditions for a civil society.

No particular public "compromise" can do justice to the fullness of Christian social teaching, any more than Paul's accommodation to imperial Rome exhausted his eschatological witness to Jesus Christ. The churches continue to be summoned to embody in their own activities the present reality of God's coming new age, even as they equip their members for appropriate forms of public responsibility. The individualism-universalism dialectic defines not simply the internal dynamics of ecclesial existence, but also the complex, multi-faceted patterns of the church's relation to human societies. The church

---

52. The qualification is not universal. Michael Novak comes close to identifying the freedom in free enterprise with basic human and civil liberties. Thus, liberal democracy and capitalism are not distinct yet parallel systems of interaction, but political and economic variants of the same system. See Novak, *The Spirit of Democratic Capitalism* (New York: Simon and Schuster, 1982; reprint, Lanham, MD: University Press of America, 1991).

is charged with maintaining its radical vision in hope while in sobriety it also honors the relative good of those institutional arrangements that continue to provide order for human social existence.

Conclusion

The churches' participation in a complex, multi-faceted, ecumenical and interfaith discourse within the public arena will not restore the Christian unity of civilization, nor will it promote a Holy Commonwealth. Still less will it advance the Christianization of America or of America's basic social institutions. Compared to these comprehensive visions of world-historical importance, it is "messy," partial, ambiguous, limited. It shares the central characteristics of policy making in a democratic society: "muddling through." Yet this model may offer the most fitting way for faithful Christians to offer a social witness within contemporary American society.

Chapter 3

Christian Social Ethics as a
Theological Discipline

*E*dward Farley has heightened our consciousness of the difficulties contemporary theological faculties have in providing a credible rationale for their enterprise.[1] These difficulties have two principal sources. To begin with, there has been a proliferation of specialized subdisciplines within theological studies. These subdisciplines have, quite rightly, made systematic use of various companion disciplines in the academy in pursuing their inquiries. Inevitably, they bear the stamp of the materials and methods they use. In the midst of such a multiplicity of approaches, however, it is no longer clear that work within the theological specialties amounts to the critical investigation of a common subject matter.

At the same time, there is growing awareness in the university of the plurality of religious communities and subcommunities within the contemporary world. Not infrequently, these communities have significantly differing sensibilities about what constitutes authentic religious existence. As a result, they do not easily converse with one another about shared or overlapping concerns. Given this state of affairs, theology appears by its nature to be tradition specific and hence incapable of encompassing within a single academic enterprise a constructive interest in the beliefs and practices of multiple religious traditions.

Because of multiple critical investigations and multiple views of religious existence, theology is on the verge of disintegrating as an identifiable field of knowledge. Not surprisingly, religious studies, which are largely forms of social and cultural studies, increasingly replace theological studies in the university.

---

1. See Edward Farley's two major studies of this problem: *Theologia: The Fragmentation and Unity of Theological Education* (Philadelphia: Fortress Press, 1983), and *The Fragility of Knowledge: Theological Education in the Church and the University* (Philadelphia: Fortress Press, 1988).

The Place of Specialization in Theological Studies

In this essay I will not attempt to resolve the problems of the unity and integrity of theology, still less to meet the challenge of establishing critical theological inquiries that cut across diverse religious perspectives. My interest is more restricted. I wish to offer a way of thinking about specialization within theological studies that might simultaneously advance our insight into theology as a proper subject matter for the contemporary university. More specifically, I will provide an account of Christian social ethics as a theological discipline and suggest how work in this subspecialty might contribute to theological studies as a whole.

In effect, I will be affirming the importance of specialization within theological studies and also insisting upon the necessity of linking such studies to identifiable religious traditions. Although these developments may have complicated our attempts to conceive of theology as a genuine field of knowledge appropriate for the university, they are not, I would contend, the root causes of our problems. Rather, those causes have to do with the difficulty of sustaining credible public understandings of religion in secular and religiously plural societies.

Christian Social Ethics as a Vantage Point on Theology

My basic thesis is that the various theological specialties are not components or subdivisions of theological study, but rather distinctive vantage points on the subject matter of theology envisioned as a whole. On the one hand, none of the several vantage points has privileged standing in relation to the others, for none can finally grasp conceptually what constitutes the whole. In this respect, the whole is more apprehended than comprehended. On the other hand, some sense of the whole is presupposed if not explicitly stated in any adequate articulation of the subdisciplines of theology. Consequently, focused attention on any one of the subspecialties has the potential of significantly enriching, modifying, or perhaps qualifying all facets of theological study.

As far as I can see, moreover, there is no fixed number of subspecialties that might complete the spectrum of theological studies. Rather, there are as many or as few subspecialties as may prove practically illuminating in the quest for theological understanding. For that matter, there are no clear and fixed boundaries that properly separate the subspecialties within theology, nor can any subgroup of scholars legitimately claim exclusive rights to the critical study of particular materials. Students of theology continually cross existing boundaries among theological subfields when such a move serves a particular investigation. They do so quite properly, provided they exercise due regard for prior critical accomplishments within the subfields they enter. Thus limitations on the number of theological subspecialties and delineations of their proper boundaries are more practical than theoretical.[2]

For this view of specialization, the twin problems of the unity and integrity of theological studies reside not simply in the interfaces of the several sub-specialties within theology. They are already present within the subspecialties themselves. Each of the subspecialties requires for its own critical investigations a conception of the distinctive subject matter of theology. Without such a conception, it cannot establish itself as a form of theological study. But once the subspecialties are adequately grasped as forms of theological study, then their relations to one another need not be so problematic. Moreover, insofar as we can successfully identify the distinctive subject matter of theology, we will be in a better position to construct manageable frames of reference for attending critically to multiple patterns of religious existence in the contemporary world.

What then is the subject matter of theology? How shall we identify and explicate it? Farley's proposals are promising. In the most general terms, he suggests, theology has to do with the divine mysteries that undergird and suffuse the universe. We can attend to these mysteries, however, only as they are manifest to human awareness and as human beings are responsive to them in concrete forms of religious life. In Christian contexts, this responsiveness is

---

2. This portrayal of theological knowledge and its subspecialties is informed by the concept of perspective in perceptual experience. In perception, we can intuit an object only from a particular, finite perspective. Though we may continually adopt new perspectives on the same object, allowing additional facets to appear to awareness, we can do so only by letting go those appearances that were available to previous perspectives. Each perspective allows some features of the object to show themselves while simultaneously obscuring or concealing others. Though some perspectives may be more illuminating than others, allowing an object to appear to its best advantage, no one perspective finally enjoys precedence over the others. Nor can any one perspective furnish the conditions of the others.

At the same time, each of the finite perspectives includes an apprehension of the whole that goes beyond what we actually perceive. We convey this sense of the whole by means of language, even though our linguistic utterances both surpass and fall short of what is, strictly speaking, given to perception. I have in mind language that describes the uses of an object or perhaps articulates our relations to it. Yet the whole is already present to each of the discrete perspectives, at least in the awareness of a receding horizon at the boundaries of the various perspectives. This horizon draws us toward future possible perceptions and enables us to hold in memory previous perceptions. It permits us to recognize the multiple perspectives as perspectives on one and the same reality. Finite perspective, infinite whole—these dimensions of awareness constitute an indissoluble dialectic of perception and understanding. It is this dialectic that guides my treatment of specialization within theological studies.

This account draws upon Paul Ricoeur's discussion of the fallibility of human knowing, embracing "finitude of perspective" and "the infinity of the verb" (the latter bearing the meaning of what is perceived). Imagination mediates between the two, Ricoeur suggests. However, imagination is fallible, ever subject to faultedness. Though it permits a holistic apprehension of what is given to awareness, it tempts us to con-

called "faith," conceived as an all-encompassing way of existing in the world. Theology, then, is the "wisdom and critical reflection attending faith."[3]

Because of its orientation to the elemental mysteries of the universe, Farley rightly observes, the subject matter of theology cannot be conceived as a specifiable segment of reality. Unlike the sciences, for example, theology cannot be located on a "world territorial map" of scholarly disciplines, each of which occupies itself with some portion of reality. It is more akin to philosophy, because it concerns itself with matters that bear upon all aspects of existence.[4] In effect, theology is for Farley a vantage point on the whole of reality. My intention here is to extend his claim to the subspecialties of theology as well. The subspecialties themselves are not segments of theology, but rather particular ways of articulating the mysteries with which theology is occupied. They seek to relate those mysteries to certain facets of experience or patterns of acting or lines of thinking or modes of creativity within the worldly existence of concrete communities of faith.

If Christian ethics is to be grasped as a theological subspecialty, then we must specify its distinctive ways of attending to the divine mysteries that awaken and sustain faith existence. Christian ethical inquiries, I would contend, focus on human accountabilities for the well-being of the creaturely realm. Historically, these inquiries have highlighted human well-being within a context of accountability to God. In a twentieth-century context, however, we can no longer take for granted the viability of the natural environment. Our collective activities profoundly impact the earth's capacities to sustain life of all sorts, not human life alone. Consequently, our ethical reflections embrace our accountabilities for the earth's ecosystem as well.

The theological substance of Christian ethics stems from the fact that we interpret and assess our human accountabilities in terms of the divine mysteries

---

fuse our finite perspectives with the infinite whole, or alternatively, to lose the whole in the finite perspectives, reducing the latter to discrete and unrelated phenomena. The former is the flaw of idealism; the latter, of radical empiricism. Ricoeur's discussion has direct relevance to the problematic of this paper. In theology, finite perspective is confused with the whole when one of the theological subspecialties, most often systematic theology, presumes to grasp the whole and to lay the definitive foundation for all other subspecialties. The whole disintegrates into the multiplicity of perspectives when the latter are reduced to isolated and discrete inquiries. As an example of such disintegration, we might attempt a historical reconstruction of the origins of the Christian movement without any consideration of whether and how such a reconstruction might constitute theological inquiry.

See Paul Ricoeur, *Fallible Man: Philosophy of the Will,* pt. 2, trans. Charles Kelbley (Chicago: Henry Regnery, 1965), 26–71.

3. The phrase is Farley's. See *The Fragility of Knowledge,* 133.

4. Ibid., 118. I also concur with Farley that we can no longer view theology as the systematic ordering of revealed truth, in the manner of pre-Enlightenment theologies. For Farley's critique of the "house of authority," see pp. 124–28.

manifest to faith. Indeed, for a Christian perspective, such accountabilities are integral features of our responsiveness to those mysteries. To apprehend aright the divine mysteries is not to become preoccupied with God or caught up in the contemplation of God in isolation from our ongoing involvements with the world; rather, it is to discover ourselves both empowered and summoned by God in accountability for the world and its well-being. It is to take delight in our fellow human beings in the context of the divine life; it is to enter with them into covenants of mutual regard and care in terms of our covenant with God. Likewise, it is to relish the earth and its beauty as the creation of God even as we use its resources for our subsistence, all the while honoring the earth's limits and protecting the conditions for its continual renewal.[5]

The ethical interest in human accountabilities before God and our fellow creatures, then, is of a piece with our recognition of God's beauty, trustworthiness, and compassion. It conveys our sense of being drawn toward the mysteries of God in faith existence as we strive to live up to the moral claims that rest upon us as creatures of God.

Unfolding the Structure of Theology in Christian Ethics

In concert with Farley, I have portrayed theology as critical reflection on the wisdom and understanding accompanying faith existence. I have argued that Christian ethics is not a subsection of such reflection, but rather a distinctive vantage point on the mysteries that establish faith existence. This vantage point concerns the totality of those mysteries and also the totality of faith existence, but in terms of their bearing on human accountabilities for creaturely well-being. Consequently, there is no aspect of theological study that does not play a role in Christian ethics insofar as it bears upon those accountabilities. In turn, attention to these accountabilities has implications for vantage points represented in the other theological subspecialties.

How then are we to unpack the various aspects of human accountabilities

---

5. John Wesley's portrayal of the relation of law and gospel expresses the intimate connection of the ethical interest in human accountabilities with the theological interest in faith's recognition of God and trust in God. There is no contrariety at all, Wesley argues, between law and gospel. The very same words, considered in different respects, belong both to law and gospel. Considered as commandments, they are law; considered as promises, they are gospel. Thus, the commands to love God, to love our neighbors, to be meek or holy are but "covered" promises of God, promises that God will enable and empower our love and holiness. By the same token, the promises of the gospel, promises of forgiveness, freedom, joy, and love, convey imperatives to live in accord with that which is offered. See John Wesley, "Upon Our Lord's Sermon on the Mount. Discourse the Fifth. Matthew 5:17–20," Sermon 25 in *The Works of John Wesley: Sermons I,* ed. Albert C. Outler (Nashville: Abingdon Press, 1984), 554–55.

that belong to the faith existence of Christians? Like Farley, I would note that faith's ways of existing are borne by religious traditions that shape the life and thought of communities of faith enduring over time. These traditions govern our manner of being in the world as persons of faith. In turn, our appropriation of formative religious traditions is conditioned by our social and cultural involvements, both within the communities of faith to which we belong, but also in the larger societies of which we are a part. In more concrete terms, therefore, the task of theology is to interpret and mediate authentic traditions of faith existence in their bearing on the communal practice of concrete communities of faith in contemporary social worlds.

With this set of understandings, theological inquiries consist essentially in interpretative activities of various sorts. This insight has led Farley to suggest that the structure of theology can best be displayed by describing its constituent modes of interpreting. He attempts to unfold that structure by identifying the modalities of interpretation that encompass the primary facets of faith existence. Actually, these modalities belong to life situations as such. As Farley puts it, "faith is not a discrete life situation but a way of being in life situations."[6] Farley's proposal is that the modalities of interpretation might outline the basic structures of theological inquiry.[7]

In structuring work in Christian social ethics, I will follow Farley's attempt to identify modalities of interpretation that compose faith existence, though I am not at all points in full agreement with his specific account of those modes. There is, however, one basic difference in my approach. Farley appears to view the modes of interpretation as possible ways of delineating the subspecialties within theology. Because I consider the subspecialties as vantage points on the whole of theology, I view these modes of interpretation as operative within each of the subspecialties. Thus, instead of ordering relations among the subspecialties, they guide critical investigations within them.

In principle, the same modes of interpretation should be manifest within all subspecialties, though perhaps with different weightings depending upon the

6. Farley, *The Fragility of Knowledge,* 137.

7. Farley identifies five elemental modes of interpretation that articulate the meaning of faith (ibid., 138–42). The first three, I would suggest, make explicit the distinctive character of faith existence: (1) the critical mediation of formative traditions; (2) the constructive articulation of those traditions as disclosing something true; and (3) the appropriation of the traditions in concrete practice. The remaining modes highlight the situatedness of faith existence in the life of the world: (4) the interpretation of situations; and (5) the interpretation of vocations as primary determinants of social location.

Farley on occasion refers to the first three modes as elemental and the last three as synthetic. In my view, the latter modes do not so much synthesize elemental modes as articulate the concrete context of faith existence. Accounts of faith existence without that context are abstract.

controlling cognitive interests. In practice, we do not need to establish a definitive account of the relevant modes of interpretation before using Farley's
fruitful suggestion. My attempt here will be to elaborate the modes of interpretation most pertinent to studies in Christian social ethics and to show how
they might structure those studies. Further inquiries will disclose the value of
this effort for the other subspecialties.

When we begin to unfold the structures that order ethical inquiries, two
modalities of interpretation stand out, one relating to the practical activity
of human beings and the other to social situations. These two modalities
are intimately interconnected. On the one hand, practical human activity
always occurs in concrete social and cultural situations, which means that
it is ordered by institutions, social movements, their organizational expressions, and by the offices and roles we fill within these various processes.
On the other hand, our interest in situations is governed by our accountabilities. We seek faithful yet realistic ways of acting in concrete social situations that will promote creaturely well-being in accordance with the
divine promises.

In what follows, I will outline the interests that govern these two modalities of interpretation in Christian social ethics. I will also indicate how other
modalities of interpretation crucial to theology come into play. The interest is
to establish Christian social ethics as theological inquiry and to show its
import for all aspects of theological study.

Practical Human Activity: The Structures of
Moral Accountability in Faith Existence

The accent on accountability in Christian ethics presupposes that we are capable of more or less independent action, that for better or worse our actions
have consequences for the creaturely realm, and, finally, that our actions are
subject to a valuative assessment, as congruent with or contrary to the
promises accorded faith existence.

In my previous work, I have drawn upon phenomenological studies to formulate a theory of action that displays the moral significance of action. I used
this theory as an interpretative guide for the critical appropriation of moral
understandings contained in classic Christian traditions.[8] If sound, however,

---

8. See my *The Use of the Bible in Christian Ethics* (Philadelphia: Fortress Press, 1983), 15–28. See
also chaps. 2 and 3 of my *Hospitality to the Stranger: Dimensions of Moral Understanding* (Philadelphia:
Fortress Press, 1985), 35–96.

the theory should have relevance for any critical study of ethics, whether it be philosophical or theological, whether it be Christian or Jewish or Buddhist or perhaps comparative in its religious orientation. Here my intent is to develop the interest in practice in closer connection with the concrete social situations that organize human activity, and to do so in terms of the ethical vantage point on faith existence.

The terms *practice* and *action* are somewhat interchangeable. Practice suggests the repetition, even routinization, of particular patterns of acting, perhaps until they are virtually "second nature." Action may refer to a unique response or initiative within a particular situation. Action in this latter sense requires fresh deliberation and judgment about what is to be done. Specialists in ethics have tended to give the greatest attention to unique and conflict-laden situations of choice. After all, such situations present the most interesting problems for reflection.

In most actual life situations, however, ongoing patterns of practice have by far the most importance for creaturely well-being precisely because they furnish order to everyday social interactions. However, the term *action* may also be used in reference to the basic structure of human activity, for example, in discussions of theories of action. In the latter case, it embraces both unique actions and routinized patterns of social practice.

In the structural sense just noted, Christian ethics centers in critical reflection on the moral dimensions of action. More specifically, it investigates the normative standards that regulate and guide action within the larger horizon of faith existence. Social ethics is a subdivision of Christian ethics that highlights the social contexts and forms of human action.

Action is, of course, more than its moral dimensions. Indeed, in the greater part of our day-to-day activity, the moral interest is by no means paramount. We work. We maintain the spaces where we live and work. We provide for our daily sustenance. We take part in ritual acts that maintain our relations with fellow human beings and renew a common world. We play and relax. We visit with friends. We spend time with those we love. Even actions that are central to communities of faith are not primarily moral in their import. There are liturgical acts, acts of instruction, acts of pastoral care, acts of collective deliberation about communal goals and objectives. At the same time, action of all sorts invariably has its moral dimensions, so that it is always possible to adopt a moral point of view on action.

Ethical discourse about human accountability has characteristically revolved around three sets of categories: obligations (or duties) and prohibitions, values and disvalues, and virtues and vices. These categories structure the ethical interest in human activity.

Obligations and the Conditions of Existence

Obligations and prohibitions have to do with the basic conditions of existence insofar as their effective operation is in our power. Obligations specify our responsibilities for sustaining basic life conditions. Prohibitions forbid overt actions that violate them. Obligations and prohibitions regulate human action. They define binding requirements for action that we must satisfy whatever else we might also choose to do, and they set limits to morally acceptable actions that we must honor in pursuing our various objectives. Their moral function is to sustain space for creaturely well-being insofar as the maintenance of such space is contingent on human activity. Normally, obligations and prohibitions cannot be overridden except where it can be shown that setting aside or violating a particular requirement promises in a contingent set of circumstances to further or protect the good they are designed to maintain.

For Christians, moral obligations and prohibitions enter into faith existence as divine commands or imperatives. They are integral features of a covenant of grace first offered by God to Israel. This same covenant was subsequently renewed in Jesus Christ in the face of persistent human failures and violations. In its renewal, the promises of the covenant were extended to all humankind. In that extension, they assumed diverse forms in multiple social and cultural settings. Christians hope for the ultimate completion of an all-encompassing covenantal communion, when God becomes "all and in all."

Theological themes do not simply provide divine sanction for obligations and prohibitions to which human beings are already subject, as though their function were simply to undergird human motivation to moral responsibility. By firmly placing the moral life within an environment of grace, these themes profoundly impact the character, scope, and even the content of the moral life. They transform the anxious delineation of rights and obligations into generosity and trust, the giving and receiving of life in the unfolding rhythms of grace. They point to the fulfillment of moral obligation in enjoyment—the enjoyment of all creatures of the earth in the context of our enjoyment of God.

Because their function is essentially regulative, obligations and prohibitions cannot exhaust the substance of the moral life. Their role is to protect the fundamental moral conditions of creaturely existence. They are, as it were, guardians of the boundaries of such existence: what must be done, what may not be done. Our everyday discourse discloses limitations in the simple two-value logic of these basic categories. To convey our moral sensibilities about various sorts of actions, we frequently turn to a range of intermediate expressions poised somewhere between the straightforward obligation and the unequivocal prohibition. These intermediate expressions furnish imprecise yet finely nuanced gradations of judgment for the moral assessment of action.

On the positive side, there is a scale of actions that are urged, praised, commended, desired, normally expected, approved, though not, strictly speaking, commanded or required. On the negative side, there is a contrasting scale of actions that are fully accepted (almost as though they were morally indifferent), permitted (though hardly praised), tolerated (usually with some discomfort), disapproved, and finally, actively discouraged, though not yet altogether prohibited. These gradations point to the second set of moral categories, those articulating values and disvalues. It is the latter that fill in the moral substance of these intermediary terms in guiding human activity.

Values and the Substantive Goals of Action

The second set of moral considerations is directed to the telos of existence. It conveys our aspiration after the fullness of creaturely well-being, again, insofar as it can be affected by our actions. It facilitates our reflections on the total meaning of action, embracing yet surpassing the more precisely defined regulative principles. Indeed, it identifies the ends that the regulative principles ultimately serve. These latter considerations are expressed as values and disvalues.

Values are notions that display, both for ourselves and others, what we conceive to be good about various realities, processes, or states of affairs in our world. Values are essentially ideas, not concrete realities. They express the purposes served by human action. In so doing, they furnish action its motivating ground. It is in reference to our value priorities that we justify particular action choices. In situations of choice, we adopt courses of action likely to result in outcomes that favor the values we prize. Disvalues in contrast convey what we judge to be bad about various realities in our world. The latter we seek to avoid or diminish. (The term *evil* is probably better seen as the negation or perversion of basic obligations and prohibitions because it does not so readily admit to gradations, despite our talk of "lesser evils.")

Value is not exclusively a moral term.[9] Indeed, there are as many sorts of values as there are regions of experience where we distinguish good or bad, better or worse. Values have to do with qualitative comparisons among various kinds of realities. As one identifiable value-type among others, moral

---

9. For my account of values and my proposal for a constructive value theory, cf. *Hospitality to the Stranger,* 66–92.

values are associated with the integrity of persons, groups, communities, whole societies, and finally, a comprehensive world order.

A moral perspective on values concerns a comprehensive ordering of values. It involves discriminating judgments about value relationships. Through critical reflection, we strive for value harmonies—values that mutually enrich one another and that resist polluting disvalues. We also face up to value conflicts with difficult trade-offs, for example, a long, healthy life on an even keel versus a shorter life full of uncertainties but with highly pleasurable gratifications. Many values that offer attractive life possibilities are, of course, essentially incompatible. We then have to decide what matters most, thereby rejecting arrangements that jeopardize our more encompassing sense of the good.

A moral ordering of values specifies a pattern of life that promises fulfillment to human beings in their personal and communal existence. In Christian ethics, such an encompassing vision is characteristically conveyed in primal images— the coming realm of God, the beloved community, the realization of God's shalom—or perhaps by way of abstract concepts such as justice, freedom, peace. Constructive work in Christian ethics, therefore, consists of critical interpretations of such notions in their bearing on a normative ordering of values.

Unlike obligations and prohibitions, which refer directly to specific kinds of actions, values concern situations, processes, or states of affairs that are the likely consequences of human actions. In this respect, they are related to action only indirectly, by way of the anticipated ends of action. This indirection is a reminder that the substantive goods we seek are not altogether in our control. We can state the point more strongly: no matter how carefully we plan and calculate, we cannot fully predict the outcome of our actions, especially in complex social situations. Indeed, the more complex the situation, the less we are able to predict or control what will follow from what we do. And when it comes to our grand, encompassing visions of creaturely well-being, we are often unable to devise any practical courses of action likely to promote the good we seek.

In practical planning, values have the greater moral import when we can translate them into measurable objectives likely to be furthered by identifiable courses of action. Even in this context, the better part of wisdom is to act in ways that themselves already embody the ends we seek; for although the ends may justify the means, it is equally the case that the means tend to determine the ends. The Christian sense of hope bestows moral significance on patient waiting and faithful enduring when no realistic ways are open for furthering God's encompassing vision for creation.

Ethical reflection on action discloses the fact that a broad interest in values is more elemental than a cognitive interest in truth, that is, simply knowing what is the case about some aspect of reality. Indeed, our value-laden involvements with the world are what generate specifically cognitive interests. It is because our valuative attachments have high importance in the economy of our lives that we urgently want to know whether and to what degree they have a basis in reality! As a cognitive notion, truth appears as one value among others in the total field of values. Universities recognize this fact when they include in their programs of study critical reflection on values and value harmonies.[10]

Morally speaking, truth is not in the first instance a cognitive matter at all. It has to do with the requisites of human discourse: the obligation to tell the truth and the prohibition against deceit or lying. The values served are authentic human communication, mutual understanding, openness, trust, community. The accompanying virtue is, of course, truthfulness, a deep-seated disposition to tell the truth.

To sum up, obligations and duties are related to the basic conditions of creaturely well-being; values and value harmonies, to the total creaturely good. As expressions of faith existence, both of these interests are directed to the goodness, beauty, and majesty of God. We should not overstate the distinction between obligations and values. The life conditions we are obliged to sustain have moral significance because they foster values we honor. Likewise, we promote certain values because we sense that we are obligated to do so. These two modes of discourse flow into each other at every point, even though they represent contrasting styles of reasoning.[11]

Virtues and the Excellencies of Moral Actors

There is a third set of moral considerations that is also crucial to practice. This set has to do with the identity and integrity of the moral actor. It specifies

---

10. This is one of the points where I may differ with Farley's view of elemental interpretative modes. Farley lifts up three notions: tradition, truth, and practice. Truth is a crucial notion for theology. We cannot complete our theological work by attending only to the existentially meaningful, as was in vogue for an earlier generation of theologians. We need to be able to show that theology concerns reality, that it is a way of attending to dimensions of reality not accessible to, let us say, empirical methods of inquiry.

Yet for theology, truth is not the most elemental mode of interpretation. It is a derivative mode, dependent upon prior valuative engagements with the world. Even for systematic theology, the prior question is not, Are Christian convictions true? It is, What are the meaning and significance of our Christian convictions for the ways in which we live in the world?

In some respects, the truth question is the most radical question we can ask. It has the potential of undermining our convictions, showing us that reality is something other than what we have supposed. In a practical sense, however, the value issues are more radical, for they present us with basic choices about how we will live our lives. I would contend, therefore, that the more elemental questions are axiological, at least for an ethical vantage point on theology.

11. In recent philosophical ethics, these types of moral interest are often discussed as deontology and consequentialism (or utilitarianism). See, for example, William K. Frankena, *Ethics*, 2d ed. (Englewood Cliffs, N.J.: Prentice-Hall, 1973,), esp. chaps. 2–4, pp. 12–78. Cf. my *The Use of the Bible in Christian Ethics*, 15–28.

strengths, cultivated through processes of maturation, that give a person the capacity for moral judgment and action. The relevant moral strengths consist of basic dispositions and attitudes that orient moral actors to concrete life situations in appropriate ways. They include skills in deliberation that reflect accumulated moral wisdom. Of special importance, however, are our developed capacities to handle our passions and feelings—our desires, our ambition, our greed, our anger, our fear—so that these drives and emotions become resources that energize morally good actions, not forces that overwhelm or thwart a moral response to the world.

In classical thought, moral considerations of this sort were articulated in a theory of virtues, that is, excellencies of character that are prerequisite to moral action.[12] In the Reformation traditions, moral strengths were interpreted as fruits of the pivotal relationships that constitute our existence as persons of faith, especially the relation with God, reflected in the transforming presence of God's Spirit in human life. In this context, virtues are not habits that an individual actor has cultivated, but rather stable accompaniments of significant relationships to which an actor is bound. In this respect, the Reformation traditions press us toward a relational theory of virtues. A major challenge to constructive thought in Christian ethics is to work out in a coherent conception the role that relationships, passions, feelings, and ongoing life disciplines have in the economy of the self's moral existence.

A theory of virtues moves us beyond the sphere of action as such to an account of human beings as moral actors. In Christian ethics, this account draws upon a broad range of theological themes, from anthropology to classical doctrines of sin, grace, forgiveness, and redemption, to ecclesiology. It uses as well contributions from developmental psychology and social psychology. Its normative content is provided by accounts of moral excellence: the self's settled dispositions to act courageously, temperately, justly, prudently; or the self's capacity to fulfill the two great commandments, the love of God and neighbor. The crucial point here is that a theory of virtues also has direct bearing on practice.[13] It concerns our accountability not just for our actions, but more fundamentally, for our character, for the kinds of persons we have become and are becoming.

---

12. Aristotle's *Nichomachaean Ethics* is, of course, the basis of this approach. It became central in Christian ethics through the thought of Thomas Aquinas. Cf. Thomas's *Summa Theologiae*, I–II, esp. questions 49–67. For a useful collection of Thomas's discussion of the virtues, see St. Thomas Aquinas, *Treatise on the Virtues*, trans. John A. Oesterle (Notre Dame: University of Notre Dame Press, 1966).

13. Stanley Hauerwas in particular has sought to show how a theory of virtues reorders the post-Kantian discussion of deontology and consequentialism. See, for example, his *The Peaceable Kingdom: A Primer in Christian Ethics* (Notre Dame: University of Notre Dame Press, 1983), 17–34.

Action presupposes concrete actors who are capable of determining their purposes and acting to achieve them. It is only as concrete actors occupying particular positions within a social system that we recognize our obligations and rank the values we prize. Commandments, laws, principles, rules, values—these notions are impotent unless concrete human beings use them as guides in responding to specific life situations. Indeed, our capacity to comprehend moral norms itself presupposes the achievement of a certain level of moral strength. We cannot grasp moral obligations that we are unable to honor in our actions; and the greater our capacities for moral action, the deeper and richer is our discernment of the moral meaning of the situations in which we find ourselves. It is as total selves that we deliberate, decide, and act. Similar points could be made about values and their promotion in human life. Thus a theory of virtues is, like theories of values and obligations, an integral part of a hermeneutic of action.

The Critical Study of Social Situations: The Concrete Context of Christian Practice

Action occurs in particular social and cultural settings. Consequently, attention to practical human activity leads to an examination of social situations. For Christian social ethics, the interest in social situations is governed by the accountabilities of faith existence. Faith existence is sustained by concrete communities that mediate authentic traditions of faith over time. It is through participation in such communities that Christians orient themselves to the wider social world. Thus Christian social thought is a fruit of the social practice of Christian churches and their affiliated associations and organizations.

The churches already belong to a social world whose composition has profoundly influenced their character. The experiences they have gained through their interactions with the larger society inform their witness to the social order and their contributions to its development. At varying levels of awareness, Christian thinkers have normally taken account of the church's social location in formulating their social thought. The critical development of Christian social ethics requires self-conscious attention to this context.[14]

---

14. This point holds for university-based theological education as well as seminary training for clergy. To be sure, one can study writings on Christian social ethics in abstraction from the social locations that sustain the thought they contain. But such work is abstract! To pursue concrete critical and constructive work in Christian social ethics, one must examine the associations that sustain a Christian social vision, that is, Christian churches. One must also attend to the social location and composition of those associations, including their relations with basic social institutions.

The task of Christian social ethics is twofold: it is to help Christian people reflect on their social roles and their realistic possibilities for influencing the direction of social evolution; and it is to discover ways in which Christians can collaborate with persons of different religious and moral orientations in working toward a shared vision of a common good. In both instances, a critical grasp of social realities is essential to studies in Christian social ethics.

Societies are historical phenomena. They have beginnings in time and unfold in particular ways in the course of their development, perhaps renewing themselves and even undergoing remarkable transformations without losing a sense of their continuity with the past. As historical phenomena, they can also grow old, lapse into decline, and eventually collapse, perhaps giving way to new social formations through interactions with more dynamic neighboring societies. Despite the broad ranges of social variation, however, societies have certain requisites that bestow common characteristics upon them. The study of society takes account of both the functional requisites of social order and their distinctive patterns of evolution over time. Christian social ethics involves, therefore, a combination of historical thinking and social analysis.

Social Analysis: The Human Sciences and Critical-Ethical Reflection

The systematic interest in the structural-functional aspects of situations stems from the fact that human societies cannot exist at all unless they are able to accomplish certain essential things in the ordering of human relationships. Societies must, for example, guarantee their members a measure of physical security, maintain conditions for the production and distribution of the means of subsistence, nurture and educate the young, and build a sense of social cohesion capable of reinforcing social requirements. Although societies can provide for these functions in an amazing variety of ways, the variety is not endless. It revolves around a relatively limited set of possibilities. The social sciences furnish a substantial body of knowledge that sheds light on basic social structures and their primary social functions.

The social sciences have not been an unmixed blessing for Christian ethics. Paradigms of empirical research initially presumed the possibility of explaining the phenomena of experience on the basis of behavioral laws. This conception of explanation implied a deterministic view of social reality. It rendered naive the belief of moralists that human action flows from subjective resolve. Indeed, for the empirical sciences action ceased to be an intelligible concept at all. Behavior became the overriding category. The prospects of scientific explanation appeared to undermine the possibility of ethics.

In order to use the sciences in social analysis, students of ethics had to clarify the nature and limits of scientific explanation, especially as applied to human behavior. This problem did not prove to be so difficult. One simply had to display the abstractness of empirical scientific research, that is, its concentration on selected features of experience considered in isolation from their concrete occurrence. One could then show that the moral point of view dealt with aspects of experience that escaped the net of scientific abstraction. As is well known, Immanuel Kant's critical philosophy provided the decisive model for this delimitation of the empirical sciences. The more difficult problem was to conceptualize within a moral point of view the contribution of the social sciences to an understanding of social reality. This latter task continues to challenge social-ethical inquiry.[15]

In general, the social sciences enable us to isolate dynamics in social existence that condition and regulate human activity. These factors constrain, channel, and even enhance action possibilities, but they do not finally determine action. In Paul Ricoeur's happy phrase, "they incline, but without necessity."[16] Consequently, although knowledge of these factors can vastly expand our comprehension of human behavior, it does not equip us, not even in principle, to give full explanations of what human beings might say and do.

We may be tempted to suggest that the sciences deal with human behavior insofar as it is shaped by antecedent causes, whereas ethics deals with human action insofar as it is subject to direction by human volition. However, such a view falsely bifurcates the self into separate compartments, the determined and the free. It fails to recognize that both scientific and ethical vantage points on action are abstractions when taken in isolation. In concrete experience, the various facets of social existence are organically interrelated, intermingling with and suffusing one another. Thus the conditioning and regulating factors that play upon action enter substantively into its actual occurrence. They affect judgment, motivation, decision making and action. In turn, our choices interact back upon these same factors, shaping their operation.

Indeed, the more we grasp how these conditioning factors function in social life, the more we are able to use them in promoting our own purposes. We take them into account in anticipating the probable actions of others, and we adapt our own projects to their operation so that they work for us rather than against us. When they seem likely to frustrate our goals, we devise strategies for minimizing their impact. Comprehension of the dynamics of human

---

15. In my judgment, Gibson Winter's study *Elements for a Social Ethic: Scientific and Ethical Perspectives on Social Process* (New York: Macmillan, 1966) still provides the most sustained and comprehensive treatment of this problem.

16. Paul Ricoeur, *Philosophie de la Volonté: Le Volontaire et L'Involontaire* (Paris: Éditions Montaigne, 1950), 85.

behavior enables us to expand the reach of our purposive activity, whereas naïveté and ignorance leave us subject to processes that consistently overwhelm us. As our powers increase, so does the scope of our accountability.

In the American context, the most influential social theories have been functional in orientation. They have focused on the identification and explication of the basic functions of society. They have used a systems model to display the interrelations of processes that provide for these functions.[17] For functional theories, social order is a phenomenon to be explained, not a taken-for-granted reality. The presumption is that social order can be maintained only if a society is reasonably successful in providing for basic social functions. Social disorganization, social disintegration, and in the worst cases, social chaos, are indications of functional failures. Such failures are taken to be the most dangerous threats to social well-being.

More recently, critical theories of society have gained prominence in the American context.[18] These theories focus on the systematic ways in which societies disadvantage or oppress certain segments of the population. Race, class, and gender have received special attention. For critical theories, order as such is not the primary interest, but an order that in freedom nourishes the full development of the capacities of the people. In this respect, a moral perspective drives critical theory to a degree that is not so obvious in functional theories. The presumption of critical theory is that societies have an extraordinary array of devices for maintaining themselves even in the face of severe functional shortcomings. The task is to discover the possibilities of humanizing social change. Such possibilities are linked to points of stress or conflict in the functional interconnections of ongoing social processes. Points of stress disclose weaknesses in the existing order that social movements might exploit in seeking a more just social order.[19]

---

17. Talcott Parsons's work represents the most ambitious recent effort at theory construction of this sort. For an overview of his approach, see Talcott Parsons and Edward A. Shils, eds., *Toward a General Theory of Action: Theoretical Foundations for the Social Sciences*, pt. 2 (New York: Harper & Row, 1951), 47–243. Parsons and Shils are the coauthors of this section. They attempt to display the distinctions and relations of personality theory, culture theory, and social theory. For a convenient summary of Parsons' application of this model to social theory, see his *Politics and Social Structure* (New York: Free Press, 1969), 5–57.

18. Jürgen Habermas has become the most influential representative of critical theory among students of Christian social ethics. Habermas locates his work within the history of social theory in his two-volume study *The Theory of Communicative Action*, trans. Thomas McCarthy (Boston: Beacon Press, 1984). For his application of this theory to the critique of advanced capitalist societies, see Jürgen Habermas, *Legitimation Crisis,* trans. Thomas McCarthy (Boston: Beacon Press, 1975).

19. Habermas identifies the key crisis of advanced capitalism as a "legitimation crisis"; that is, the value orientations of the society do not justify the social distribution of burdens and benefits. As a result, existing forms of social order lack clear legitimacy. See Habermas, *Legitimation Crisis*, 68–74.

These two types of social theory have counterparts in Christian social ethics. Classical Christian thinkers in both Catholic and Reformed traditions have tended to conceive basic institutional forms as largely given. Order has been a paramount value. The central theological and ethical issues have concerned the role Christians might properly play within established institutional structures. Social gospel and liberation traditions have been preoccupied with the injustices of human societies. They have directed their energies toward movements for social justice and liberation.

Both of these perspectives have bases in the eschatological orientation of the early Christian movement. This orientation called for a provisional acceptance of existing forms of social order despite their distortion of God's ultimate purposes. Existing social structures furnished a God-given context for the proclamation of the gospel. The eschatological orientation also constituted a summons to the faithful to enter into an alternative community over against the dominant society. This community afforded new ways of being together in the world in recognition of the nearness of God's coming realm.[20] The dialectical interplay of the old age that is passing away and the new age coming into being, Troeltsch observes, nurtured both socially conservative and socially radical tendencies. Both have persisted throughout history and continue to figure in ecumenical discussions.[21] Consequently, both functional and critical theories contribute to Christian ethical reflection on social reality.

Social Analysis: The Critical Study of Institutions and Social Movements

Structural-functional treatments of society deal with social institutions and social movements. Both belong to the realities of social existence. Institutions furnish a stable framework for human interactions; social movements are instances of collective initiative to achieve shared goals. In general, institutions provide stability, whereas social movements make up the dynamic aspects of human societies. Yet dramatic changes can be produced within stable institutional contexts, for example, changes brought about by capitalist development. Basic value systems and patterns of economic behavior may remain more or less intact through fundamental social transformations. Similarly, social movements frequently emerge that are directed toward preventing particular kinds of changes, for example, movements to protect the

---

20. See my discussion of these themes in *The Use of the Bible in Christian Ethics*, the final chapter, 177–206.

21. See, e.g., Ernst Troeltsch, *The Social Teaching of the Christian Churches* (Chicago: The University of Chicago Press; 1976), 82–86. [Reprint Louisville, Ky.: Westminster John Knox Press, 1992.]

ecology, or, to take a quite different example, groups mobilized to oppose open occupancy in suburban neighborhoods.

Social institutions are composed of deep, shared expectations regarding patterns of human interaction and structures of human relationships. These expectations are internalized in the elemental attitudes, beliefs, and dispositions of persons in the society. Through ongoing processes of socialization, they enjoy a high degree of self-evidence among members of a society. We take them for granted as "the way things are." In their self-evidence, they function as mechanisms for social control, assuring relative stability in human societies.[22] Institutional structures and processes order the principal regions of human association: economic, social, political, and cultural. They provide the context of virtually all human action. According to this schema, religious institutions have social-integrative and culture-bearing functions.

Organizations articulate basic institutional forms in more or less explicit arrangements of offices and functions, so that continuity and effectiveness are assured in activities crucial to social existence.[23] At various levels of activity, members of an organization generate policies aimed at meeting organizational objectives. In most cases, these policies emerge through well-established procedures that reflect the distribution of authority and the division of labor within an organization. Thus they are products of deliberation, judgment, and decision making. However, to gain support, both within particular organizations and in the larger society, these policies must accord with institutionalized social expectations.

Social movements reflect collective investments of human energy in the promotion of shared goals that go beyond institutionalized patterns of human activity. The goals in question may be fully compatible with primary social values. In this respect, social movements do not necessarily represent a challenge to basic social institutions. They may reinforce those institutions, for example, popular demonstrations in support of a national war effort. More broadly, social movements may express central characteristics of particular social institutions. In the American context, voluntarism has been a prominent value, reflecting fundamental ideals of liberal democracy. When American people organize themselves to address certain problems or to promote certain goals, they are acting in accord with the voluntary principle of American

---

22. For a strong presentation of the institutionalization of human interactions, see Peter L. Berger and Thomas Luckman, *The Social Construction of Reality: A Treatise in the Sociology of Knowledge* (Garden City, N.Y.: Doubleday, 1967).

23. For a theoretical treatment of organizations, in distinction from and in relation to institutions, see Amitai Etzioni, *A Comparative Analysis of Complex Organizations: On Power, Involvement, and their Correlates* (New York: Free Press, 1961). Etzioni builds upon Parsons' functional theory of society.

democracy. Social movements may, however, be directed against established social practices, even in violation of public law. Their intent could be to protest oppressive social patterns and to open the way for substantive social changes, at least at the level of policy, perhaps at a structural level as well. Examples include the abolition movement, the women's suffrage movement, the labor movement, the civil rights movement, or the current right-to-life movement.

Movements committed to social change are not necessarily radical so long as they do not call into question the organizational principles of a society.[24] American democracy has been highly stable over a long period of time precisely because it provides spaces for collective initiatives aimed at shaping specific social arrangements. The constraint on such initiatives is that their goals and methods of protest prove themselves compatible with the requirements of basic social institutions.

In some societies, normally those that fail adequately to provide the requisites of social order, social movements may become radical and then revolutionary, seeking nothing less than the overthrow of an existing social order. To be effective, social movements must themselves achieve satisfactory levels of organization, and in that organization they must draw upon the internalized expectations and shared values of participants in the movements. In this respect, such movements invariably display a measure of continuity with existing institutional arrangements.

Attention to the structural-functional aspects of situations entails examining the institutional and organizational forms at work in those situations. It includes assessments of the effectiveness of both in providing the requisites of a well-ordered society. Social movements continually play among the basic institutions of human societies, articulating their possibilities, expanding their reach, frustrating their smooth operation, reordering their priorities, perhaps transforming their fundamental values.

In social ethics, we have special interest in the consensual features of social institutions and movements. In this context, consent means that people act in accord with societal norms, not simply in response to coercive measures or out of presumptions of personal advantage, but on the basis of respect for the moral worth of those norms. Coercive force and perceptions of mutual interest are undoubtedly crucial components of social order. Yet societies require moral authority for their regulative principles if they are to

---

24. Organizational principles give specific identity to particular social formations. They consist of central social processes that regulate and limit the range of possibilities for change and development in a particular society. See Habermas, *Legitimation Crisis*, 9–10.

achieve functional effectiveness and maintain stability over time. They gain this authority from ideas widely shared in the society. Such ideas are integral features of social order.[25]

Peter Berger discusses how religious and moral ideas serve to explain and justify apparent social evils. Such ideas constitute a social theodicy; that is, they furnish an account of the social world that shows that it merits allegiance despite its manifest shortcomings. This theodicy displays the essential validity of basic social institutions; it reinforces the people's obligation to honor those in authority and to obey the rules of society; and it renders intelligible any seeming unfairness in the distribution of social benefits and burdens.[26] To be persuasive, a social theodicy must have a substantial basis in cultural materials esteemed within the society as a whole. It cannot simply be invented *ad hoc,* certainly not by those whose interest it most immediately favors. It requires roots in a rich tradition, preferably with a revered history of interpretation. The more a social theodicy participates in the central themes of a culture, the more the essential rightness of the social arrangements it sanctions enjoys self-evidence among the people.

Critical social theories proceed from the fact that the dominant religious and moral ideas of a society often sanction unjust and oppressive social systems. Then the social theodicy functions as an ideology; that is, it is composed of ideas without authentic social grounding. Such ideas conceal and distort the true realities of social existence. Their role is to protect the special interests of those who illegitimately benefit from the established order. Yet movements for social change also require moral if not religious legitimation—I would say both. Attempts to disrupt social order and to reorder social relations along different lines themselves demand justification. One must show their essential rightness and demonstrate that the suffering they cause is necessary or unavoidable or perhaps preferable to that which already exists.[27]

Building upon the insights of Karl Marx, critical social theory shows how our social locations predetermine our judgments about social reality and its normative values. For both functional and critical approaches, however, moral and religious ideas are integral to social order. The challenge is to test the alleged grounding of such ideas in social reality. It is to discern whose interests they favor and whose interests they override.

25. See Peter L. Berger, *The Sacred Canopy* (Garden City, N.Y.: Doubleday, 1969), 3–51.

26. Ibid., 55. See the whole of chap. 3, "The Problem of Theodicy."

27. Jon P. Gunnemann speaks of revolution as "change in theodicy." See his *The Moral Meaning of Revolution* (New Haven: Yale University Press, 1979), 232–46. He specifically criticizes Karl Marx's presumption that a proletarian revolution would overcome the need for a theodicy by bringing into being a realm of freedom and of human mastery over nature. See ibid., 167–68, and the whole of chap. 4.

In structural-functional terms, churches in modern, secular societies are voluntary associations. Their organizational expressions are complex, embracing local congregations, several levels of regional organizations, associations of congregational representatives, and general legislative and administrative bodies of the denominations. There are also program agencies and affiliated educational and welfare organizations within denominations, often with parallel structures in ecumenical bodies. Reflections on a Christian social witness are appropriate within each of these organizational components.

In addition to the formal arrangements that provide legitimate channels for official church pronouncements, there are innumerable subgroups, intimately linked to the churches, that offer their own distinctive social witness: caucuses, special interest groups, and issue-oriented associations. Examples include the Women's Christian Temperance Union, the Methodist Federation for Social Action, the Southern Christian Leadership Council, or Clergy and Laity Concerned About Vietnam. Such groups attest the shared convictions of individual Christians. They may function within particular congregations and denominations; they may be ecumenical and even interfaith in their reach; and they may draw people together in a common social vision without regard to explicit religious attachments. Organizations of this sort are able to take considerably stronger critical positions than are possible within representative denominational assemblies. They may attempt to enter directly into a public discourse, but they also interact back upon official church bodies, influencing their social practice. In short, both issue-oriented associations and representative church bodies play a role in the social teaching of the churches. Individual leaders in any of these contexts have special opportunities to shape conversations in Christian social ethics.

As voluntary associations, the churches have considerable freedom in activities that involve the individual choices of adherents. This freedom gives them ready access to families and neighborhoods; it permits them to sponsor and interact with other culture-bearing and human welfare institutions, such as universities and hospitals. The churches may also seek to influence economic patterns and to participate in the public life of basic political institutions. However, their access to these latter processes is more qualified. The limitations stem in part from the fact that there is a plurality of diverse religious communities whose freedom of expression must be protected. In part, however, they reflect the fact that economic and political institutions perform essential social functions that are not readily amenable to religious sensibilities.

In secular, pluralistic societies, the church's social teachings are normally able to make their way into the public arena only in conjunction with religious and moral ideas that undergird a normative social order, that is, what Troeltsch called the "civilizational ethic."[28] In the United States, the civilizational ethic consists of principles of liberal democracy and human rights. It includes normative values associated with capitalism, such as individual enterprise, self-sufficiency, and competitive acquisitiveness.[29] The civilizational ethic, Troeltsch contends, is invariably distinguishable from peculiarly Christian teaching, even in allegedly Christian societies, because it is linked to institutional structures whose underlying functions are independent of the religious impulses of the Christian message. This independence holds especially for political, legal and economic institutions. Consequently, he concludes, Christian social teachings that are capable of engaging basic social institutions on policy matters must be combined in some fashion with the reigning civilizational ethic of the society.

Any effective synthesis of Christian ideas and civilizational ethic constitutes a "compromise," that is, an adjustment of Christian teaching to the reigning norms of a society. However, such a compromise gives distinctively Christian social thought a share in the authority of the civilizational ethic. It is by way of its participation in a civilizational ethic, Troeltsch contends, that Christian teaching has been able to influence social processes and policies.

The civil rights movement of the 1960s is a case in point. When Martin Luther King Jr. lifted up the moral vision of the black churches, he spoke of the "beloved community." In making his public witness, he appealed to human rights guaranteed by the Constitution of the United States, even though these rights are characteristically interpreted in individualistic terms and hence are somewhat in tension with a Christian vision of community. King's social message was an effective compromise of Christian teaching and the American civilizational ethic. Troeltsch believed that the churches cannot continue to play a role in social evolution unless they can maintain and renew such compromises.[30] The same point holds, I would contend, for social movements, for example, revolutionary movements, in which Christians become conscientiously involved.

Studies in Christian ethics consist of the critical mediation of normative Christian traditions in concrete situations of practice. Such mediation gains pertinence and effectiveness with the aid of structural-functional analyses of

28. See Troeltsch, *Social Teaching,* 1001–1002.

29. I have elaborated these points in my essay "Renewing Ecumenical Protestant Social Teaching," in *Justice and the Holy: Essays in Honor of Walter Harrelson,* eds. Douglas A. Knight and Peter J. Paris (Atlanta: Scholars Press, 1989). [Reprinted as chapter 5 in this volume.]

30. These ideas inform Troeltsch's treatment of the entire span of Christian social thought in the West. They are succinctly pulled together in the concluding section of his *Social Teaching,* 999–1002.

social processes. Of special interest is the relation that prevailing normative ideas have to those processes. The truth question primarily concerns the degree to which reigning social ideas—Christian or otherwise—reflect awareness of the interconnections of thought and social processes. Effective reconstructions of Christian social thought contain well-founded appraisals of social realities that both facilitate and hinder a faithful Christian witness.

Historical Thinking: Uncovering the Historical Aspects of Situations

Structural-functional approaches to situations are not self-contained. They gain their significance in contexts of historical understanding. Functional necessities constrain historical developments, but it is the latter that constitute the concrete reality of the social world. Thus social situations occur as features in the ongoing movement of unique configurations of social and cultural phenomena. To grasp a situation is to know its historical trajectories.

Like structural-functional studies, historical treatments of situations in Christian social ethics are guided by the churches' own placements in larger streams of social existence. It is out of the context of the churches' involvements in struggles for justice that historical thinking gains significance in social-ethical reflection. The scholarly task is to help the churches respond to their social settings out of a critical appropriation of their normative traditions, with full awareness of their own social locations.

When we turn to the historical aspects of situations, we continue to be occupied with matters treated in structural-functional approaches. Now, however, we examine functional components of societies in terms of their development over time. We reconstruct the pivotal events that shaped their evolution. We take particular note of the traditions that sanction their activities within a social order.

The primary interest at this point is to uncover the formative meanings of situations, that is, the significations they have for human actors who are involved in them. It is by way of these significations that we have access to the concrete moral import of situations. The contention is that the interpretation of situations is in itself an activity in moral reasoning. It is an attempt to discern the pivotal moral issues that already reside in a social world. In this respect, a hermeneutic of situations must not be confused with pure empirical description, especially when the latter is carried out in abstraction from value considerations. The hermeneutical interest is to uncover the moral meanings that figure in concrete human interactions and relationships. A formal account of the moral dimensions of action furnishes guidelines for recognizing such meanings.

A perceptive grasp of the moral import of a situation does not in itself tell us how we are to respond. Virtually any situation offers a range of moral possibilities. We have to sort out and rank these possibilities in terms of our individual and collective commitments. Furthermore, many situations confront us with perplexing moral ambiguities that the most discerning reading cannot resolve. Any response we make will, consequently, reflect that ambiguity. The challenge is to find ways of reordering the relevant considerations so that moral ambiguity is reduced if not dispelled. The careful interpretation of situations does, however, orient us to the questions requiring our attention.[31] The presumption of this approach is that moral values and obligations are not purely transcendent norms residing in a realm of ideality that must somehow be imposed upon situations in order to provide moral direction to action. Although the moral norms we honor may have an ultimate religious grounding that surpasses concrete, historical realities, they belong as well to social situations as lived.

We get at the formative meanings of situations through the critical retrieval of normative traditions. We approach these traditions in terms of their role in the formation of existing situations, guided by the questions we confront in attempting to deal with those situations. In this frame of reference, tradition functions as both burden and resource, as hindrance and hope. We seek to exorcise what is destructive and to reclaim what releases and empowers.

Self-consciousness about the historicity of situations is not always highly pertinent to moral understanding. In familiar, routinized situations, historical thinking scarcely comes into play at all. The moral sense of the situation is already more or less clear, and in general we know what to do. To be sure, our moral sensibilities have gradations of urgency that shade into one another. At one pole are moral ideals recognized by most but fulfilled only by the heroic few. At the other pole are acts so reprehensible that they are unthinkable except for the emotionally disturbed, or perhaps those who belong to a criminal underclass. Ordinarily, we know what is desirable or morally urgent or obligatory; likewise, we know what is morally dubious or disapproved or strictly forbidden. We do not require a fully articulated historical self-consciousness to deal with such matters.

Historical thinking takes on urgency in periods of rapid change that weaken an established moral order. Familiar, taken-for-granted norms lose their self-evidence. Willing consent to social expectations declines; the maintenance of

---

31. See H. Richard Niebuhr, *The Responsible Self: An Essay in Christian Moral Philosophy* (New York: Harper & Row, 1963), 55–68. For my discussion of Niebuhr's proposal for an ethics of the "fitting," see *Hospitality to the Stranger*, 100–122. Niebuhr also explicates the ethics of the fitting in terms of "society" and "time and history," though with less attention to the methodological implications of attention to these phenomena.

order depends increasingly on calculations of self-interest—what can we get out of "going along"?—and on the coercive measures of the state. In such circumstances, the meaning of a situation becomes problematic, a matter to be examined and clarified. It is then quite evident, as Niebuhr argued, that the prior question is "What is going on?"[32] We strive to reorient ourselves to our situation by recounting the history that has brought us to moral crisis. We seek to estimate the possibilities for renewal in our normative traditions.

Crisis does not simply have the negative connotation of danger. It also suggests kairos, the opening up of the moment of opportunity for new creation. A social order in difficulty may reveal itself as an order of repression. Its difficulties open the way to the recovery of repressed memories and to the retrieval of neglected, even forbidden, traditions.[33] These memories and traditions place in question the taken-for-granted understandings that have previously determined the meaning of social situations. A struggle for hegemony follows, perhaps with an uncertain outcome. The reigning civilizational ethic may undergo transformation to incorporate knowledge derived from repressed traditions, thereby resulting in a new moral consensus. At the other extreme, social fragmentation may occur, with proposals for national partition and the relocation of conflicting populations as a device for restoring social order (e.g., India-Pakistan, Cyprus, Lebanon). Then again, social revolution may occur, or the hegemonic culture may reestablish itself and successfully subdue the challenger. Similar dynamics may be set in motion by increased interactions among human communities representing multiple cultures, though without necessarily implying a history of oppression.

A historical vantage point on situations becomes essential when the situations in question are dynamic and conflict laden. Under those circumstances, the moral import of a situation can come into focus only through the clash of interpretations, through intense polemical exchanges, through patient negotiations aimed at building a new moral consensus. Disputes of this kind are never purely theoretical. They involve power struggles. They occur in the crosscurrents of social, economic, and political forces. Consequently, they cannot be resolved simply by the construction of stronger, more cogent arguments, nor by a more rigorous application of the rules of evidence. They require social accommodation and reconciliation.

In complex, modern societies, a genuine moral consensus almost invariably

---

32. See Niebuhr, *The Responsible Self*, 60.
33. Drawing upon the work of Michel Foucault, Sharon D. Welch has demonstrated the usefulness of these categories for contextual understandings of theology. See in particular her discussion of "the insurrection of subjugated knowledges" in *Communities of Resistance and Solidarity: A Feminist Theology of Liberation* (Maryknoll, N.Y.: Orbis Books, 1985), 44–47.

eludes us. Such a consensus is more a moral imperative and a hope than a practical project. Normally, we have to content ourselves with compromises and trade-offs, with mutual accommodations of one sort or another that might permit us to live together in a shared world. Dealing with conflicting interpretations of important life situations becomes our ongoing pattern of moral existence. Such irreducible multiplicity is the nature of a genuinely pluralistic social order. Indeed, a key moral requirement of life in such a society is to honor diversity and, if possible, to celebrate it. Where such mutual respect cannot be sustained, threats of violence and social fragmentation are ever present.

Christian social ethics finally centers in the critical development of the social witness of the churches in their particular social situations. The questions have to do with how the churches are to place themselves among the conflicting interpretations of the social world. What do their traditions lead them to see in that world? What moral possibilities are suggested by their efforts to mediate those traditions faithfully? The churches have their distinctive traditions of social thought and practice. These traditions reflect not only social ideas associated with the gospel message, but also moral conceptions that amount to "compromises" previously accomplished with the civilizational ethic of predecessor human societies.

In secular, religiously plural societies, Christians have to develop their social vision in at least two frames of reference. They must become clear about their own witness and its grounding in fundamental faith convictions, and they must find ways of articulating their distinctive witness that are suited to a public discourse. In general, formulations of the latter sort can best be worked out through critical engagement with the reigning civilizational ethic. The civilizational ethic furnishes the moral notions that make possible a public discourse about the common good.

The churches are deeply implicated in their social situations, so that the moral conflicts of the society are replicated within their own internal life. Within the churches themselves dominant traditions of Christian thought clash with neglected and forbidden traditions, and multiple traditions reflecting the diverse social locations of the churches work against a coherent and unified Christian witness. The struggle for a common mind that faithfully expresses the church's mission is, then, an ongoing task with its own perplexities and ambiguities.[34]

---

34. I have displayed some of these complexities in my essay "Renewing Ecumenical Protestant Social Teaching."[Reprinted as chapter 5 in this volume.] In that essay, I lifted up the recent difficulties of ecumenical Protestant social teaching, specifying what would appear to be necessary to accomplish its renewal in contemporary American society.

Conclusion

The subfields of theology, I have been contending, are particular vantage points on the divine mysteries that awaken and sustain faith existence. Christian ethics deals with faith existence in terms of our accountabilities for creaturely well-being. Critical reflection on these accountabilities focuses on the personal and communal practice of Christians in concrete social situations. Such practice includes Christian contributions to a public discourse about a well-ordered society. Assessing Christian practice embraces both the critical mediation of normative traditions that provide guidance for action and also the critical assessment of the moral significance of existing situations of action. The latter requires a productive combination of historical thinking and social analysis. The intent is to discover realistic possibilities for social action that accord with divine promises given to faith existence. Where fidelity is sustained within the social practice of the Christian churches, inquiries proper to Christian social ethics can make substantive contributions to the total theological enterprise.

Chapter 4

Corporate Capitalism and the Common Good

A Framework for Addressing the Challenges of a Global Economy

Christian churches face formidable challenges when they strive to articulate a social witness that is both authentically grounded in distinctively Christian understandings and also capable of constructively engaging the ongoing operations of complex societal systems. Even when particular forms of social organization reflect historic Christian influences, for example, Puritan contributions to the formation of constitutional democracies, such structures still depend for their operational effectiveness on foundational principles that operate in relative independence of the Gospel message. Strictly speaking, there is no such thing as a Christian society, not even as a utopian vision. Indeed, the Puritan example is itself quite exceptional. In more typical cases, the Christian witness has consisted of attempts to achieve realistic yet substantive reforms in existing states of affairs, so that higher levels of justice and greater human compassion might be realized within an established social order.

To gain practical importance, Christian social teaching must encompass critical investigations of the patterns of organization that constitute concrete societal systems. There are at least two major steps to this undertaking. First, we must uncover the basic structures and operational dynamics that render particular societal systems effective in performing essential social, economic, and political functions. Jürgen Habermas refers to these structures and the processes they facilitate as a society's "organizational principles" (1975, 7–17). These principles furnish the requisite conditions for collaborative human action within a given society. They also limit the kinds of interactions that are realistically possible in that society. Second, we must identify the shared values and the normative moral standards that are ingredient in the systems under study. In significant measure, all societies depend for their stability upon the willingness of their members to observe the basic ground rules of social order. These ground rules set boundaries for acceptable human practices, and they specify duties that are mandatory for reliable social functioning. In a similar fashion, particular societal systems invariably privilege some value complexes over others in measuring social well-being. The favored values serve as guidelines for decision making within the primary spheres of social life. Christian social teaching involves a continuous search for fruitful ways of combining social dimensions of the Gospel message with normative understandings that configure particular patterns of collective human activity. It is by critically shaping and creatively enriching reigning civilizational values that Christian teaching plays a constructive role in human social life (see Parsons 1969, 5–57; Ogletree 1991).

To address contemporary issues, Christian teaching must come to grips with the operations of free-market economies. Because of the pervasive impact of an expanding global economy on virtually every aspect of human life, there is no longer any social concern of importance that does not involve economic realities as well. We must, therefore, gain a fuller grasp of the organizational principles that make free-market economies such powerful forces in human life. Free-market economies enable many good things to happen. They stimulate productive efficiency and material abundance, and they foster conditions that reinforce basic human liberties. Yet they produce harm as well, in particular, the exploitation of low-skilled workers, and environmental damage. They also give rise to vast inequalities of income and wealth that marginalize disadvantaged members of society. These harmful tendencies are difficult to contain, however, because they are directly linked to factors that render free-market economies effective in the first place. If a free-market economy is to serve a broader human good, substantial public oversight is required. What complicates this claim is that government interventions in economic activity can themselves lead to unintended negative consequences, often doing more harm than good. The challenge is to devise procedures for containing destructive tendencies inherent in market economies without at the same time undermining their strengths.

The Direct Benefits of Free-Market Economies

Fostering Productive Efficiency and Economic Growth

The most obvious benefits of a free-market economy reside in its efficiency, its capacity to produce for human consumption a generous supply of goods and services. Abundance does not guarantee fairness in the allocation of resources, nor equal opportunities for all. Still less does it presume that individuals will exercise sound judgment in pursuing their personal preferences.

What abundance does assure are material resources sufficient to sustain human life in a world of scarcity (see Benne 1981, 126–35, and Wogaman 1986, 58–67). As population growth stretches environmental limits, this accomplishment is scarcely minor in its import for the common good.

In free-market economies, business enterprises secure profits by delivering goods and offering services that are both responsive to consumer "demand" and capable of generating income from sales that exceeds production and delivery costs. To survive in a competitive environment, businesses must at least be able to match the performances of other firms. Equally important, they must constantly adapt their own activities to changing market conditions. They pursue these goals by prudent capital investment in the "factors of production"—the extraction of raw materials; the construction of facilities; the design and acquisition of equipment used in producing and distributing consumer goods, including advanced communications technologies; and the employment of human labor. Capital investment has three primary objectives: (1) to increase productivity, enabling fewer workers to accomplish more with similar efforts; (2) to improve the quality and marketability of goods and services in response to consumer demand; and (3) to develop new products and services that promise strong market appeal.

Within a market context, profitability is a measure of satisfactory performance and a requisite for long-term viability. Indeed, profit-making corporations are morally obliged to deliver profits to shareholders who have invested in their operations. When a corporation consistently fails to achieve satisfactory results, the value of its stock will fall. If it cannot restructure its operations in a manner that will reverse these losses, it will either be taken over by a more successful firm, or it will go bankrupt. Strong incentives toward capital investment in productive efficiency are, therefore, central features of a market economy. In recent decades, chief executive officers, board members, and major shareholders have, by a wide margin, been the primary beneficiaries of corporate success, though high-ranking managerial and technical staff and outside contractors may themselves have received significant portions of the profits—in salaries, sales commissions, stock options, and payments for services. Lower paid employees will at least have had jobs with pay, though with a declining share of the nation's income and wealth.

Market Equilibrium and the Cultivation of Mutual Interests

The desired outcome for a free-market economy is "market equilibrium." Market equilibrium refers to a relatively stable balance between product supply and consumer demand. If supply exceeds demand, prices will fall, forcing producers and retailers to cut prices below profitable levels in order to "clear" inventories. If demand exceeds supply, prices will rise until adequate supplies can be generated. Similar dynamics operate in all sorts of market exchanges, affecting prices, fees, interest rates, royalties, wages, salaries, benefits, and the like. When fluctuations in supply and demand are confined to specific products and services in particular sectors of the economy, they are routine features of market dynamics. Thus, shrewd consumers regularly anticipate department store sales as seasons of the year come to an end. Skilled corporate managers strive to adjust product supply to match anticipated consumer demand, and if possible, to reduce the time required for the production and delivery of consumer products, so that smaller inventories become feasible.

At the aggregate level, market equilibrium concerns patterns that impact the economy as a whole. Rapid economic growth can stimulate an inflationary spiral in prices, wages, and overall production costs. Sooner or later, an overheated economy will "crash," unless timely means can be employed to slow the pace of growth. In contrast, a stagnant economy evokes widespread caution, leading to declines in consumer spending and corporate investment, the principal engines of economic growth. Declines in salaries and wages, stock values, and employment levels will follow. The result will be a recession unless means can be found to stimulate the economy. Advanced economies rely on government fiscal policies to stabilize economic growth. To stimulate a stagnant economy, public spending may be increased and taxes reduced. To cool an overheated economy, reverse measures may be pursued: reduced public spending, commitments to pay down public debts, even tax increases (see Keynes 1973). The U.S. Federal Reserve Bank responds to swings in market cycles by adjusting interest rates for overnight lending to banks, a measure that influences the cost of credit in the economy as a whole. Higher interest rates slow the rate of economic growth by increasing the cost of borrowing; lower rates stimulate economic growth by encouraging borrowing for corporate investment and consumer spending (see Heilbroner and Thurow 1998, 143–52). Given the inherent volatility of markets, equilibrium is not a state that can be routinely maintained, even in the best of times. It rather serves as a measure of optimal economic performance, one that informs Federal Reserve policies, government initiatives, and the financial management of businesses and corporations.

Market equilibrium also refers to mutually satisfactory exchanges among participants in market activity: producers or retailers and their consumers; professionals, agents, or consultants and their clients; corporations and their investors; employers and their employees; lenders and their creditors. The underlying presumption is that market activity is driven by the desires of rational, self-interested individuals to maximize "utilities," that is, to secure goods and services that promise a fuller and more satisfying human life. Consumers seek such utilities by acquiring affordable goods and services in the market; profit-making enterprises gain profits by providing desired utilities at prices that exceed production and delivery costs while also remaining both attractive and affordable to consumers. Some of the profits will be invested toward future enhancements in productivity; another portion may be distributed among shareholders, enabling them to secure their own desired "utilities." Thus, the individual self-interests of producers and consumers connect in the marketplace, to the mutual advantage of both.

In the global arena, market exchanges can cultivate more positive relationships between national states that on security grounds alone would not be natural allies. Nations with mutual economic interests have stronger incentives to work together, and a greater determination to resolve potential disputes in a peaceful manner. The European Economic Community, for example, is progressively uniting people who were once mortal enemies. Similarly, expanding trade relations could enable the U.S. and China to move beyond the enmity of the Korean and Vietnam wars, and to resolve continuing strains over the status of Taiwan. Indeed, China is on the verge of new cooperative relationships with all of the major partners in the World Trade Organization. World trade hardly solves all problems; in fact, it offers nations with advanced economies new opportunities to dominate and exploit nations whose economies are still in the early stages of development. Fears of domination by multinational corporations, many of which are based in the United States, account for popular resistance to free trade. Here as well the benefits and liabilities of market economies are linked together.

Attention to mutual interests formed in market exchanges requires us to qualify the classic contention that market dynamics are wholly determined by individual drives to maximize utilities. Self-interest is certainly pertinent to market operations, and its impact is largely benign so long as it is strictly confined to bona fide market exchanges. Nonetheless, it is a vast oversimplification to presume that autonomous individuals can achieve mutually satisfactory outcomes simply by shrewdly coordinating their own interests with what they perceive to be the interests of others. Markets function most efficiently when business enterprises are genuinely committed to customer satisfaction, and when consumers fully intend to meet their payment obligations. The principle of mutuality, I would suggest, funds the ethical dimensions of market exchanges. It displays the importance of truthfulness and reliability in such exchanges: the full disclosure of information pertinent to an exchange, the refusal to market products that are unsafe, or to deceive and mislead potential customers in order to make a sale. To engage in practices that violate standards of truthfulness and reliability is not only immoral; in the long run, it is imprudent as well. If markets are to work effectively, individual self-interests must be circumscribed within moral boundaries that are themselves essential to market operations (see Finn 1996, 2002). It follows that principles of corporate ethics are by no means alien impositions on market processes. They articulate commitments that enhance market exchanges (see Krueger et al. 1997). Corporate responsibility begins with fiduciary responsibilities to shareholders, but it includes as well fair and honest dealings with clients and customers. Standards of this kind normally require backing in public law, so that all profit-making enterprises are held accountable to the same ground rules in their business practices. Where such law is lacking, deceit, fraud, unreliable services, and faulty or dangerous products can become widespread, seriously inhibiting free-market exchanges. In turn, public law must itself be reinforced by a broader moral ethos, one that can only be maintained through human bonds formed in non-market associations.[1] Corporate ethics, public law, and the moral resources of a greater human community undergird conditions essential to fruitful market exchanges (see Novak 1982, 171–87).

Similar points can be made about employer-employee relationships. Proprietorships and partnerships in particular often flourish by cultivating a team spirit, one that fosters mutual respect and active collaboration in the pursuit of shared goals. Even larger corporations benefit by actively promoting a wholesome workplace, one that honors all employees as persons of dignity and worth. Conscientious corporations vigilantly strive to prevent all forms of employee abuse, especially by supervisors and senior executives. However, equilibrium is far more elusive in the labor market. It presumes that corporate employers have an adequate supply of qualified workers to meet their production goals. Likewise, employees themselves, both actual and potential, must have meaningful employment options so that they can negotiate satisfactory terms of employment. Employees with skills in high demand are usually well positioned for such negotiations. Indeed, during the 1990s, corporate executives, working in close collaboration with corporate boards, managed to secure extraordinarily lucrative compensation packages. These packages did not always track corporate performance, nor did they manifestly serve legitimate corporate interests.

---

1. Alexis de Toqueville's portrayal of the new American Republic remains the classic source of this insight (1969). See also Bellah 1975, Mooney 1989, and Putnam 2000.

Where low-skilled workers are involved, the market balance shifts in the opposite direction. Because low-skilled workers have few meaningful options, they often face desperate choices: employment at wages too low for a decent life, or no job at all. The accent on labor markets presumes that low-skilled workers more or less receive what they deserve based on their contributions to production processes. Besides, dissatisfied workers are allegedly free to secure additional training if they wish to improve their employment options. Alternatively, they can support union organizing and rely upon union leaders to bargain on their behalf for more satisfactory employment contracts. Outcomes that satisfy unions may in turn pose threats to the efficiency and profitability of the firms involved, giving them incentives to relocate or at least to "outsource" portions of the productive process. In either case, at least one, and perhaps both, of the parties will be dissatisfied with the outcome. Market turbulence implies, moreover, that workers and employees at all levels of the corporate ladder must constantly be prepared to adapt to ever-changing economic circumstances. Otherwise, they will simply be left behind.

Success in the market inevitably involves risks, especially in regard to capital investments in future productivity. The classical warning, *caveat emptor* or "let the buyer beware," retains its validity insofar as it highlights these risk factors. However, when this warning implies the absence of any credible bases for mutual trust, it seriously impedes market operations. All parties are then burdened with the task of scrutinizing every detail of a possible transaction. The myth of an "invisible hand" cannot overcome these difficulties.[2]

Aggregate Measures of Economic Performance

Where efficiency and growth are the focus of attention, standard assessments of economic performance give primacy to aggregate measures, in particular, gross domestic product (GDP), with little or no attention to disparities of income and wealth that might exist within a total population. GDP includes consumer spending, corporate investment, income from exports reduced by expenditures for imports, and government spending for public goods and services. Government spending that merely "transfers" income within the population is not included—Social Security, Medicare, Medicaid, food stamps, health care for children in impoverished families, Temporary Aid to Needy

---

2. The metaphor of an "invisible hand" originated with Adam Smith. However, it was by no means central to his vision. It was casually mentioned one time in *The Wealth of Nations* in a discussion of imports (1776: IV, 2, 9). It was also used once in *The Theory of Moral Sentiments* (1790, IV, 1, 10). The latter book stressed the moral sentiments that bind people together, the eighteenth century equivalent of "civil society."

Families (TANF), the Earned Income Tax Credit (EITC). Transfers are omitted because they do not contribute to economic growth. They may even divert resources from investments or consumption that would have stimulated growth. Consumer spending by beneficiaries of government transfers does count within GDP.[3]

The preoccupation with GDP tacitly presumes that all people will be affected, for better or worse, by the aggregate state of the economy. To the degree that aggregate growth does benefit all members of a society, then even the "least advantaged" could conceivably be better off in an efficient and growing economy than in a centrally planned economy that was egalitarian yet stagnant (see Rawls 1993, 6). However, standard assessments of economic performance involve no claims about the welfare of the least advantaged, nor do they display interest in a "fair" distribution of resources. Productive efficiency and aggregate growth represent the overriding values. Corresponding philosophical defenses of this priority stress "desert" over notions of "fairness" or concerns for the "least advanced" in a rationally credible theory of justice (Nozick 1974; Sher 1987). By devoting considerable energy to measuring inequalities in income and wealth, "welfare economists," such as Arthur Okun or Amartya Sen, move outside of the mainstream of their discipline. Yet welfare economists have not themselves been able to demonstrate convincingly that distributional variations as such have any direct bearing on a society's economic performance (see Sen 1997, 142–48; see also Arrow 1963, Atkinson 1983, Okun 1975, Thurow 1975). Consequently, a focus on inequality amounts to a shift of attention from strictly economic performance to broader measures of social welfare. Societies with fully developed free-market economies differ fundamentally from societies with "zero sum" economies. In the latter, concerns for aggregate growth are subordinated to priorities such as state sovereignty, the maintenance of an established class and status system, or the implementation of egalitarian principles in the distribution of income, wealth, and opportunity (see Thurow 1980).

3. Heilbroner and Thurow 1998, 77–80, call attention to important deficiencies in GDP. GDP does not adequately discount for inflation. It makes some adjustment for quality improvements in manufactured goods, but ignores improvements in services, such as ATM machines or computer enhancements of data management. Yet services now make up 70% of the U.S. GDP. GDP has traditionally divided productive activity into agriculture, mining, construction, manufacturing, and services. Services, however, are no longer a homogeneous sector, ranging from health care and investment bankers to waitresses in fast-food chains. GDP makes no distinctions regarding the ultimate uses of public expenditures, whether for education or for prisons. Education could properly be called "investment in human capital" rather than a form of "consumption." Finally, GDP does not discount for environmental harm or social deterioration, nor does it distinguish defensive spending (locks, burglar alarms) from positive acquisitions (automobiles). Because of the usefulness of comparisons across time, there is resistance to reconstructing GDP. Still the former focus on Gross National Product has been redirected to GDP to take account of the global economy.

Apart from special commitments associated with membership in monastic, Anabaptist, and utopian communities, Christian teachings on social justice have not typically pressed for strict equality in the distribution of income and wealth. Advocates of Christian socialism and of some liberation theologies would represent an exception to this pattern (see Novak 1982, 239–71; Hicks 2000, 140–96). More typically, Christian social thought has emphasized a special concern for the "least advantaged," embodied in the compelling phrase, "preferential option for the poor."

Inequalities are considered acceptable provided they are integral to social states that, relatively speaking, benefit the least advantaged members of society. The "preferential option" clearly obligates us to give sustained attention to distributional patterns in assessing human well-being in societies that have market economies. Wide and growing disparities in income and wealth, either within a given nation or a wider global context, evoke serious concerns, for they place at risk basic commitments to honor the dignity and worth of all peoples.[4] Aggregate economic performance is pertinent to social well-being, but it cannot suffice as a satisfactory measure of social achievement. We require as well comprehensive studies of human well-being.

Market Incentives for Social Practices That Produce Harmful Results

While market incentives for productive efficiency, technological innovation, and economic growth can have enormously beneficial outcomes, they inevitably produce socially harmful consequences as well. Of central importance are the persistent pressures to cut production and delivery costs, both by exploiting low-skilled labor and by "externalizing" the burdens of industrial pollution. There are also strong incentives to develop environmentally harmful consumer goods.

The Exploitation of Labor

Corporate profitability depends upon success in holding production costs to a minimum. The cost of labor is a key variable in this undertaking. Savings are achieved by technical advances in equipment that is used in the production and delivery of consumer goods. These advances increase worker productivity, so that fewer workers can accomplish equal or greater results with the

---

4. Daniel H. Weinberg 1996, 1, notes that between 1968 and 1994 income inequalities in the U.S. have increased by 23% for families, and 18% for households (1996, 1). See Hicks 2000, 5.

same effort. They also bring about a division of labor, breaking complex operations into simple tasks that workers with limited skills can perform. The goal is to tap into a supply of laborers who urgently need jobs, but have few qualifications that would give them meaningful employment options. Such persons would be desperate enough to accept employment at low wages with no guarantees of either job security or basic health and retirement benefits. This imbalance of power between employers and employees virtually assures the exploitation of workers, especially when it becomes standard practice within industrial and commercial firms.

Karl Marx argues that the lowest sustainable wage is the cost of "labor power" itself. In Marx's usage, labor power refers to the worker's capacity to produce in contrast to what he or she actually produces. The cost of labor power, therefore, is the amount a worker requires to stay alive, and to maintain sufficient energy to work productively (1967, 177–98). This cost would vary for different workers, depending upon their age, physical size, and general health conditions. The cost of labor power would often exceed the current U.S. minimum wage, either for individuals who must support themselves fully, or for single parents with dependent children. Among other things, a minimum wage is seldom accompanied by health and retirement benefits, still less by guarantees of job security. For the "least advantaged," moreover, available jobs are frequently located at some distance from affordable housing. Accordingly, wages would have to be discounted by transportation costs.[5] The cost of labor power would in any case fall short of John Ryan's more generous standard of a "living wage," that is, a wage sufficient to sustain a worker and his family at a level of decency (1996, 112–25).[6] Marx's analysis helps us understand the special appeal that child labor has for industrial capitalism. Reasonably healthy children can perform many useful tasks; prior to puberty, they consume less, they can be controlled by firm discipline, and they may have some parental support as well.

A market economy gives profit-making enterprises strong incentives to

5. The federal minimum wage in 2001 is $5.25 per hour. Assuming a forty-hour week, and fifty-two weeks of employment, a minimum wage would produce an annual income of $10,920. Social Security taxes would reduce this amount by $863, leaving $10,057, or $838 per month, for food, clothing, shelter, transportation, and pharmaceutical products in case of illness or injury. A single adult could probably survive on that amount, especially by dining in soup kitchens, perhaps by living in homeless shelters. One could also acquire discarded clothing and shoes from charitable organizations. A single parent with minor children would in addition have access to food stamps, Medicaid, and possibly the Earned Income Tax Credit.

6. For Ryan, it is important to add, a living wage still falls short of a just wage, that is, pay that corresponds to a worker's actual contribution to the production process. Ryan does not tell us how to measure this contribution, but he clearly is not content to let the market determine what a person's labor is worth (1996, 126–35).

foster conditions that will assure abundant supplies of cheap labor. Karl Marx described this phenomenon as the drive to build an "industrial reserve army," that is, workers who can be employed at low wages during times of market expansion, but who can be laid off with impunity during a declining business cycle (1967, 628–39). Marx had in mind non-unionized workers who have no employment contracts. The presence of labor reserves can even eliminate corporate concerns about worker safety. Workers who become ill or suffer injuries can simply be replaced.

To assure an abundant supply of cheap labor, the United States government has traditionally encouraged immigration. If workers are to be exploited, it is socially more acceptable to exploit immigrant workers, especially immigrants who have ethnic roots and religious backgrounds different from those typically found in the dominant classes. Late in the nineteenth century, a large Protestant majority with British ancestry was not particularly concerned about hardships endured by Roman Catholic workers from southern Italy. It was even more tolerable to exploit freed African slaves. Accordingly, some firms, though by no means all, welcomed the migration of African-Americans from the rural South to northern industrial cities. New industries in southern states also readily employed former slaves and their descendants.

In the United States and in Western Europe, the exploitation of industrial workers was not effectively reversed until workers managed to organize themselves into unions, so that they could bargain collectively for decent wages, reasonable hours of employment, safe working conditions, and basic health and retirement benefits. With backing in public law, unions were able, little by little, to define the "core labor values" that are essential to the common good. American corporations adjusted to these new realities so long as the market economy was largely confined to national boundaries, a condition easily maintained during two world wars and the early years of the cold war. Public interest in stemming the tide of immigrants also increased during this period, for immigrants no longer promised significant benefits for major industrial firms. Equally important, immigration laws specified that the composition of future immigrant populations would have to conform to the ethnic makeup of the U.S. population, ensuring continued social and cultural stability (see Wilbanks 1996, 25–92). For the most part, organized labor shared the public opposition to open borders, and it did not initially welcome workers of African descent. Immigrants and descendants of former slaves were viewed as competitors for available jobs.

Improvements in transportation and communications technologies, coupled with expanding global markets in a post–Cold War era, have now reopened corporate access to cheap labor. To avoid labor-union wages, industrial firms have moved significant portions of their productive activity beyond U.S. borders, where supplies of low-skilled labor are plentiful. In turn industrial decline in the United States has seriously weakened industrial unions, virtually eliminating their influence in public affairs. Service unions continue to have some impact, especially the Teamsters. Yet workers who provide services have more difficulty organizing unions, for the work they perform is often widely distributed. We are reenacting on a global level patterns that were pervasive during early industrial development.

Environmental Harm

The competitive drive to reduce production and delivery costs also leads to environmental harm. The most blatant forms of damage are well known: air and water pollution; toxic wastes; the incremental exhaustion of non-renewable resources; and the destruction of animal habitats, endangering entire species. More recently, consciousness has increased about global warming and a diminished ozone layer. The sheer size of the human population is itself a factor in environmental harm, for population growth increases pressures to overuse natural resources, with long-term negative consequences. Environmental damage is not simply a result of industrial production. It is also exacerbated by modern consumer goods. With the help of public utilities, private residences are supplied with electricity, fuel oil, and natural gas, and with telephone lines, internet connections, and cable TV. Gas and electric appliances are standard household equipment, and private motor vehicles with internal combustion engines are the primary means of transportation. Industrial capitalism has not only transformed production processes; it has radically altered the lifestyles of consumers as well, especially those in the middle and upper classes. A majority of the people living in the new industrial order have gained a stake in its continued effectiveness, despite the environmental dangers it poses.

Economists take account of damage to the natural environment by speaking of "externalities" and their neighborhood effects. Externalities are widely distributed consequences of productive activity, both negative and positive. No one is burdened or benefited by these consequences unless large numbers of people, perhaps all who live in a given region, are simultaneously burdened or benefited. Thus, water pollution burdens virtually everyone in a region, not merely the industries that pollute. There are no economic incentives for corporations to bear the costs required to correct the problem. Steps to limit pollution simply have no direct bearing on short-term market interests in efficiency, growth, and profitability. Consequently, environmental harm constitutes a "market failure," that is, a problem that competitive markets cannot effectively address by themselves. While short-term measures of aggregate economic performance may appear satisfactory even without discounting for the cumulative effects of environmental harm, such harm still portends staggering long-term costs. This point holds especially for "pervasive" externalities, such as global warming.[7]

Market Failures and Public Goods

The concept of "market failures" also embraces highly valued social "goods" that, because of their "neighborhood effects," cannot be supplied through market mechanisms alone. The prominent examples include education, transportation, energy, communications, waste disposal, public sanitation, public health, and, of course, public order and national defense. It is possible in principle to have private education, private toll roads, private railways, private air-traffic control, private utilities, private telephone companies, even private security systems and weapons industries. However, a well-ordered society requires that these goods be universally available, a state of affairs that cannot be sustained without significant government involvement. Utilizing income from taxes, some government agency at federal, state, or local levels provides the goods and services in question, or it subsidizes, supplements, and closely regulates private enterprises that contribute to those goods. To take advantage of market efficiencies, government agencies properly explore ways of privatizing portions of the programs that deliver public goods. Yet a crucial government role remains indispensable.

Indirect Benefits of Free-Market Economies

Free-market economies do not simply reorder the ways in which goods and services are produced and exchanged within human societies. They have indirect social, cultural, and political consequences as well. In assessing the contributions capitalism might make to the common good, therefore, we must examine its benefits and liabilities within a larger societal framework.

Milton Friedman reminds us that capitalism is not simply about efficiency and growth in the production of wealth. At a more profound level, it is about

---

7. To assess the costs of environmental harm, Daly and Cobb have proposed an "Index of Sustainable Economic Welfare" (1994, 443–507). In this index they distinguish between "localized" externalities and "pervasive" ones, such as global warming.

human freedom, a fundamental human right (1982: 12; see Sen 1982, 81–84, 282–99). Individuals have equal rights to develop and employ their capabilities in light of their own priorities; to organize and participate actively in voluntary associations or corporate enterprises in pursuit of shared goals; and to exercise civil liberties in public life. Friedman's claim is that market freedoms are indispensable components of these basic liberties, with consequences for democratic governance and civil society as well.

Democratic States and Market Freedom

Friedman recognizes that capitalism cannot itself establish and sustain the social conditions of freedom. Government must maintain national security and public order; it must protect property rights and enforce contract law; it must furnish a monetary system to facilitate market exchanges; and it must provide essential public goods to correct against inevitable "market failures" (1982, 25–27).[8] Cass Sunstein states Friedman's point more forcefully. Markets, he argues, are not some manifestation of the natural order of things. They are "legal constructs." As such, they must be evaluated in terms of their import for human well-being (1997, 8, 348–83). At the same time, capitalism requires a principle of limited government. Limited government opens social spaces for individuals to pursue their visions of truly good and fulfilling human lives, so long as those visions do not violate or jeopardize the rights of others.

It is possible for societies to institute democratic states—with free elections, limited terms of office, even a division of powers within government—while also maintaining a centrally planned economy. Indeed, precisely because of their commitments to economic justice, Christians have often advocated some version of democratic socialism as the optimal societal system. Similarly, it is possible for highly centralized and authoritarian states to open specific sectors of the economy to market activity, in particular, the manufacturing of selected products for export in a global market. Yet the full benefits of capitalism require a democratic state with limited powers, so that market transactions can

8. The surprising omission is the lack of any reference to "corporate law." By creating an "artificial person," corporate law protects officers, board members, and investors from liability for corporate actions. At the same time, it requires "transparency," so that potential investors can be reasonably well informed about the financial status of a given corporation. The latter is indispensable for a flourishing stock market (see Romano 1993). Friedman's primary interest, however, is to oppose widespread forms of government involvement in the economy that he finds objectionable: price supports, tariffs, import restrictions, control of output, rent control, price and wage controls, minimum wages, price caps, detailed regulation of industries, licensure provisions, but also Social Security, public housing, national parks, public toll roads (1982, 35–36).

be shielded from improper government intrusion. When constitutional limits on the powers of state are fully established, only compelling public reasons can warrant interventions in the economy, which belongs to the private sector. The economy is best served, moreover, when any necessary government involvements are themselves implemented in ways that are broadly compatible with market operations. Otherwise, government initiatives will collide with incentives that energize markets in the first place.

Similarly, market freedoms, though in themselves distinct from political freedoms, can indirectly reinforce political freedoms and basic human rights as well. An authoritarian state that permits a limited amount of free-market activity will have increasing difficulty suppressing other expressions of freedom as well. Accordingly, democratic states may be justified in promoting free trade with highly centralized, authoritarian states even when such states pursue policies that violate human rights.[9] Free trade fosters conditions favorable to democratic freedoms. On the other hand, even a democratic state that controls the primary business and industrial affairs of society will inevitably limit basic political freedoms as well. When economic and political power are heavily concentrated in government offices, then state power can impede citizen initiatives. Given these complex interconnections, there are solid grounds for linking democracy and capitalism in a concept of democratic capitalism (see Novak 1982).

Freedom and Civil Society

Market freedoms open pathways to social mobility, undermining established class and status systems that in earlier generations severely limited the life chances of the people. By attracting immigrant populations seeking a better life, advanced capitalist societies steadily become more diverse—ethnically, racially, and culturally. Increased mobility and population diversity diminish the authority of established religious and moral traditions, releasing people to think for themselves as they strive to determine the values that will govern their life practices. Thus, the full realization of freedom gives rise to a wide plurality of beliefs and practices, so that a highly cohesive and unified social-cultural system can no longer be sustained.

Human beings have not ceased to be social creatures. In a world of free-

---

9. The data on these claims are mixed. China, for example, shows signs of tightening state constraints on the freedoms of its citizens. Yet the necessities for such constraints are strongly felt by current rulers precisely because of market influences. In any case, it is unrealistic to expect sweeping changes in a short period of time.

dom, however, the implementation of human sociality depends substantially upon concrete human choices. These choices define the nature and scope of intimate relationships among consenting adults. They encompass mutual commitments by like-minded persons to form organizations and associations that support shared convictions about life's meaning and purpose, including churches, synagogues, mosques, and temples. Unique and irreplaceable persons freely participate in a wide range of complex, dynamic, and ever-changing patterns of human interaction while continuously transcending and transforming those patterns in creative and imaginative ways. It is through multiple networks of independent yet overlapping human associations that the bonds of civil society are fostered, providing a measure of stability and a sense of shared responsibility for the basic institutions of society. Ideally these bonds will bestow authority on what John Rawls calls a "thin" theory of the good, that is, a basic framework of normative moral principles that will enable diverse human beings to coordinate their activities fruitfully within the economic and political arenas of society, but that will also release them to pursue their own more comprehensive visions of truly good and fulfilling human lives (1971, 302; 1993, 273–74). Thus, the common good resides not simply in values that citizens hold in common; it also embraces socially shared commitments to honor the freedoms of individuals and groups to determine for themselves how they shall live their lives. The problem is that groups marginalized for one reason or another may not be fully included in this fragile network of free associations, so that they are effectively denied meaningful participation in civil society.

Where individual freedoms enjoy privileged standing among widely shared values in a society, we can anticipate that social upheavals and destabilizing shifts in social values will be a recurring phenomenon. In effect, the inherent turbulence of market economies translates into social and cultural turbulence as well, rendering more difficult the sustenance of a broad moral consensus within society. With constantly shifting populations, moreover, churches, synagogues, and mosques must continually renew and reconstruct themselves if they are to maintain their vitality. The negotiation of differences, creative adjustments to new developments, and the resolution of conflicts among various organizations, associations, and communities within the larger society become vitally important processes for maintaining social stability. The expansion of freedom is manifestly not without social risks. Yet freedom does foster an environment that encourages creative human initiatives, and it heightens individual accountability for social well-being, values that are not incompatible with distinctively Christian celebrations of freedom. The challenge is to incorporate the more fluid and open-textured notion of "civil society" into Christian understandings of community, thereby moving beyond classic conceptions of the organic cohesiveness of human societies, conceptions which sanctify social stability and order above other values. In civil society, living with difference and change is a normal state of affairs.

Market Distortions of Political and Civil Communities

While market freedoms do reinforce basic human liberties, the growing weight of economic forces in social life tempts us to view virtually all goods as commensurable "utilities" that are accessible through some form of mutually satisfactory exchange. In effect, every good has a price, and all human interactions are about the efforts of self-interested individuals to "maximize utilities" in pursuing their personal preferences. The term "commodification" is widely used to articulate this tendency, with the aim of reminding us that many human goods cannot and must not be bought and sold in the market place (see Anderson 1993, 168–69). I would highlight two expressions of this tendency: distortions of political processes in democratic government, and the marginalization of persons who have not had meaningful opportunities to equip themselves for full participation in the economic and political affairs of modern societies.

Market Freedoms and Political Freedom

I have noted basic interconnections between free markets and democratic government. On the one hand, democratic government establishes the legal conditions that make free markets possible. On the other hand, free markets indirectly reinforce basic human liberties, including the civil liberties of citizens. Yet it is equally important to hold clearly in view the fundamental differences between market freedoms and democratic freedoms (see Walzer 1983). While democratic governments must be responsive to individual and group interests, their primary purpose is to sustain a framework within which public discourse about the common good can take place. Such discourse presupposes shared values and mutual commitments that dispose individuals, private associations, even profit-making corporations, to look beyond their own narrow interests toward a broader common good. These broader commitments are dependent for their effectiveness upon the continuous nurture and renewal of "civil society."

As a matter of principle, democracy guarantees all citizens a voice in public discourse about the common good, without regard to their social status or their personal conceptions of a truly fulfilling human life. Special interests play important roles in political debates. Individuals and organized groups have rights to protect their own interests against improper government intrusion, or against violations by other persons and groups living in society. They also have rights to seek public support for their activities when those activities legitimately merit consideration as "public goods," for example, government subsidies for the fine arts or for scientific research. In practice, political debates rarely produce a new consensus about the public good. The more likely outcome is rather some aggregation of diverse and even competing interests, a compromise that satisfies no one completely, but that remains acceptable within the body politic. Thus, coalitions of profit-making enterprises are in tune with the democratic process when they join forces to promote their special interests, particularly when they can plausibly argue that their interests are compatible with a broader public good. Distortions emerge, however, when the public arena becomes the political equivalent of a competitive market, and personal or corporate wealth is employed to promote narrow special interests over against the interests of others, as though some "invisible hand" would assure a mutually satisfactory outcome. Public law and public policies never function simply as structures that allocate "utilities" designed to satisfy individual preferences. They concern practices that necessarily affect the whole of the society, directly or indirectly, for better or for worse. Equally important, one cannot simply walk away from unsatisfactory political outcomes, as one might exit a market that offers no marginally attractive exchanges. The losers have to live with the results regardless of how they view them.

In newly emerging democracies, distortions of political processes commonly involve bribes and overt collusion between elite factions and public officials. Such blatant corruption has from time to time marred the American story as well, especially at state and local levels, though effective law enforcement has largely eliminated corruption as a major threat to our political system. In contemporary American politics, the impact of a "wealth effect" is more subtle, finding primary expression in the escalating costs of political campaigns, especially at the federal level (see Corrado 2000). By contributing generously to political parties and political action committees (PACS), corporate officers gain privileged access to legislators and public officials, who respond by approving narrowly focused legislation or budgetary adjustments that are oriented to the special interests of contributing corporations—targeted tax breaks, government subsidies, relief from existing regulatory constraints, tariff protections.[10] Corporate gains from campaign contributions

---

10. Wealthy individuals also use generous campaign contributions to gain access to public leaders. Yet individual wealth invariably has corporate links of some sort, reflecting stock portfolios or personal ties to particular industrial and commercial enterprises.

substantially exceed their initial costs. Consequently, support for election campaigns is manifestly a prudent corporate "investment." Exchanges of this kind are also self-replicating. Once the benefits of corporate contributions become manifest, corporations that had not previously been politically active recognize the importance of becoming more involved. Similarly, as corporate contributions increase the resources available for federal elections, potential candidates for public office realize that their prospects for success will largely depend upon their fund-raising skills. They also know that successful fund raising requires good personal relationships with corporate representatives. In the strict sense, there may be no violation of current federal election laws, but the appearance of corruption remains, endangering the integrity of the political system.

Market Freedoms and Human Capabilities

Market freedoms reinforce basic human liberties for those who have had opportunities to develop their capabilities. However, given vast and growing disparities of income and wealth in the United States, many who grow up in poverty never have the support systems and educational resources they require in order to realize their potential. Government programs, such as "Head Start," do exist that are designed to support "at risk" children, but existing resources are far too limited to address the problems adequately. It is hardly surprising that children raised in poverty perform poorly on standardized tests, or that they see few chances for living satisfying and fulfilling human lives. Surveying the dismal life prospects that surround them, many turn in despair to the underground economy, to drugs, prostitution, petty theft, even crimes of violence. To counteract these developments, the primary public response over the last decade has been more vigorous law enforcement, often involving some version of racial profiling, with severe mandatory sentences for drug-related offenses. Among nations with fully developed free-market economies, the United States now ranks first in the size of its prison population!

If freedom is a fundamental right, then a society founded upon freedom is obliged to see that all persons have meaningful opportunities to cultivate their natural abilities, so that they can exercise the liberties to which they are entitled. Vulnerable people cannot simply be abandoned to despair when they are unable to support themselves in existing labor markets. John Rawls underscores this point in his theory of justice, insisting that all persons must be granted *"fair* equality of opportunity" to pursue their personal visions of truly fulfilling human lives (emphasis mine). In other words, a purely formal insistence on the absence of external constraints will not satisfy the principle of equal opportunity (1971, 302; 1993, 6). True fairness requires public resources in order to assure quality education for all, beginning with preschool and continuing at least through undergraduate studies in colleges and universities. Fairness also encompasses guarantees of basic health-care for children, and subsidized child support services for working parents. Market incentives can in some measure reinforce public commitments to human development. Friedman notes, for example, the broad social benefits that flow from public provision of basic education for all. He further observes that deficient levels of investment in "human capital" is a persisting "market failure" in free-market economies. Therefore, he favors government-guaranteed loans for vocational and professional training, recognizing that the recipients of such opportunities will be its primary beneficiaries (1982, 86–88, 98–100, 104–7).

Social commitments to freedom and opportunity for all citizens finally depend, however, upon mutual human commitments fostered in civil society. It is these ties that undergird broader human concerns for a common good that promises fair equality of opportunity for all people. I have noted persisting weaknesses in the contemporary American version of civil society, in particular, the fact that all sub-groups within the society are not fully embraced within the network of overlapping associations that constitute civil society. This limitation especially affects public attitudes toward many of the poor who have been left behind. It tempts us to disregard their needs unless there is demand for labor that they could provide. In its deadliest forms, racism is now manifest through the class system, reinforcing a public readiness to abandon many of the poor in favor of more pressing priorities. Christian social teaching obliges us to resist these tendencies, with emphasis on the dignity and worth of all human beings.

Within a global context, Amartya Sen and Martha Nussbaum are pressing international organizations to give priority in their planning to programs that equip people to develop their own capabilities over programs designed to meet basic human needs (Sen 1999, 282–99; Nussbaum 2000, 96–100). The latter are hardly unimportant, but direct aid by itself can foster dependency, unintentionally replicating conditions that created the needs in the first place. A focus on the development of capabilities offers people new opportunities to take charge of their own lives. The visions of Sen and Nussbaum are themselves compatible with free-market economies. They presume human responsibilities to work productively and to be self-supporting. At a deeper level, they stress the capacity of human beings to claim their freedom as "agents," that is, beings who can decide and act for themselves. For Sen and Nussbaum, agency is not a mere "means" for achieving some other end; it is an intrinsic good. Agency must figure prominently, therefore, in any adequate theory of the common good. Accordingly, a just society will foster public policies that ensure all people realistic chances to develop their capabilities.

Public Oversight of Free-Market Economies

I have been arguing that free-market economies, despite their enormously positive benefits, have harmful social tendencies that are integrally linked to the dynamics that render them effective in the first place. Indeed, the creative and destructive forces are so closely connected that we cannot easily contain the latter without simultaneously disrupting the former. Nonetheless, it is now widely recognized that government policies must in some fashion oversee and regulate market processes for the sake of a broader public good. Continuing controversies primarily concern the nature and extent of appropriate government involvements. It is important to hold in view the differing intentions that guide two basic types of intervention: on the one hand, public policies that actually facilitate market transactions, even when they are procedurally intrusive; and, on the other hand, public policies designed to protect goods which largely fall outside of short-term market interests. I have noted examples of the former: requirements for transparency, mandates for safe products, prohibitions of misleading advertising. Anti-trust law falls within this group as well. Its purpose is to ensure a competitive market place, protecting space for creative new entrepreneurial ventures. I have emphasized negative effects of market economies that largely fall outside of the immediate interests of profit-making enterprises: the exploitation of labor, environmental harm, the virtual abandonment of the least advantaged, inclinations to view virtually all human interactions, including political involvements, as variants of market exchanges. I would contend that profit-making enterprises themselves have a stake in matters such as these, for flourishing markets do presuppose high levels of social and cultural stability. At the same time, long-term considerations of this nature cannot easily be integrated into corporate planning where short-term results have such overriding importance. Consequently, corporate resistance to public attempts to address these problems is predictable. It is also appropriate in the sense that the burden of proof for government intervention in the private sector rests with government.

Advanced capitalist societies have all accumulated substantial experience with government efforts to address problems generated by free markets. What we have learned is that government interventions, no matter how well intended, can themselves have undesirable consequences, at times doing more harm than good. Cass Sunstein directs special attention to problems associated with "command and control" regulatory regimens managed by federal agencies (1997, 277–83). He recognizes that centralized regulatory procedures are necessary for addressing some issues, for example, restrictions on dangerous products, protections for basic human rights, and uniform responses to problems with national impact (1997, 337–45). In contrast to "command and control" systems, he commends policies that emphasize "disclosure and education," "financial incentives," and "decentralization." Equally important, public policies must themselves be subjected to continual review to assess their effectiveness. Where the public good is our concern, we require more than worthy goals. We require a proven record of concrete outcomes that at least approximate the goals which initially bestowed moral substance on those policies.

Public Disclosure of the Breadth and Depth of Poverty

To display the import of these claims, I would narrow my focus to policies that explicitly exemplify the "preferential option for the poor." To begin with, full public information on the nature, scope, and depth of human poverty is vitally important. Sunstein calls attention to the prominence given to GDP in assessing aggregate economic performance. He argues that we need a comparable "Quality of Life Report," one that consolidates current information on such things as consumer price index, the poverty line, income distribution by quintiles, average weekly earnings, unemployment, the extent of exposure to violent crime, life expectancy, and educational attainment. He cites as a possible model the *Human Development Index,* published annually since 1990 by the United Nations Development Programme (see O'Connor 2002; Hicks 2000).[11] The measures lifted up by Sunstein are already available in an array of government reports, especially the annual *Economic Report of the President.* Sunstein's point is that we require a single report with a high public profile, one that integrates measures pertinent to the "Quality of Life." An effective public response to the needs of the least advantaged at least requires widespread awareness of the magnitude and depth of poverty, and of its

11. Douglas A. Hicks notes that earlier HDI reports did not consider "distributional questions," focusing instead on national averages for various measures: income, life expectancy, education. To correct against this deficiency, Hicks proposed an "inequality adjusted" *Human Development Index, IAHDI* (see Hicks 2000, 215–30, 257–60). Recent *HDIs* do contain a Human Poverty Index, which measures the percent of a population deprived of basic capabilities. Yet Hicks's more comprehensive proposal still merits serious consideration.

harmful effects on human well-being. A public conscious of these realities will not so readily push aside the needs of the poor.[12]

Educational Reform: Helping Persons Develop Their Capabilities

I would underscore the congruence of understandings reflected in Friedman's emphasis on freedom as a fundamental right, Rawls's insistence on fair equality of opportunity, and the priority that Sen and Nussbaum give to human capabilities and agency in human development. These ideas are fully in accord with Christian emphases on human dignity, including the notion that productive work is a practical expression of our "calling" in Christ. They underscore the point that universal access to quality education is both a basic human entitlement, and a public good of fundamental importance.

In terms of the "preferential option," there is no public commitment more urgent than the renewal and transformation of failing public schools in poor inner-city neighborhoods. Ronald J. Sider examines the many factors that contribute to these failures: a lack of adequate funding, dilapidated facilities, unsafe neighborhoods, insufficient library resources, the absence of computer equipment, large classes, teachers who are less than fully qualified, low expectations for student performance, a substantial number of undisciplined and poorly motivated students from dysfunctional homes, bureaucratic controls that stifle teacher initiative and creativity (1999, 156–71). Given the complexity of the issues, Sider wisely resists any comprehensive proposals, though he does offer a set of principles to guide planning. He underscores the urgency of substantial public funding for education at federal and state levels, with reduced reliance on local property taxes. He argues for smaller schools; for competition among schools, both public and private; for reduced bureaucratic control; and for parental choice of schools. The intent is to create strong performance incentives for both teachers and administrators. He is open to a strategy that relies primarily on school "vouchers," provided all families with incomes at 150% to 200% of the poverty line are covered, and provided that families below the poverty line receive an additional subsidy. Sider's basic proposal, however, is for a multi-billion-dollar government commitment at state and federal levels to fund massive five-year experiments in educational reform in two dozen inner-city school districts. Approximately

---

12. Sunstein calls attention to the "Measures of Economic Welfare" (MEW) proposed by Nordhaus and Tobin (1973), and the "Index for Sustainable Economic Welfare" (ISEW), developed by Daly and Cobb (1994, 443–507). ISEW discounts GDP by considering the long-term economic impact on the environment. For more sustained study of the nature and extent of poverty, see Wilson (1987) and Blank (1997, 1992).

half of the funding would be devoted to experiments with "vouchers," and half to ventures in public school reform. Careful studies of the outcomes of the various experiments would then provide guidelines for future planning. Thus, Sider's proposal embraces several of Sunstein's recommendations regarding alternatives to "command and control" regulations by federal agencies: disclosure, the use of economic incentives, decentralization, though without releasing the federal government from accountability, and cost-benefit analyses of the results (see Sunstein 1997, 277–83). The commitment Sider calls for is substantial, but as Friedman has observed, the positive "neighborhood" effects of investments in basic education are also substantial. Among other things, they could in time yield significant savings in public funding presently allocated for law enforcement, the criminal justice system, and prison maintenance.

Along with educational opportunity, the preferential option for the poor obligates us to take steps to assure a "living wage" for all workers who must support themselves and their families (see Ryan 1996, 112–25). Because increases in the minimum wage often result in increased unemployment, our best strategy would probably be an expansion of the Earned Income Tax Credit. The EITC was designed to facilitate movement from welfare to employment. The tax credit supplements earnings up to a certain level. This level could be based on John Ryan's concept of a living wage. Persons eligible for the credit should also be covered by Medicaid. Granted, these are "income transfers." Their advantage is that they place no special burden on profit-making enterprises as such, but rather enable such enterprises to participate in processes that can enhance the productivity of low-skilled laborers. Indeed, the provision of such a tax credit might be designed to give profit-making enterprises incentives to expand opportunities for employees to enhance their own workplace skills. Finally, we must recognize that there will always be persons who cannot sustain themselves. We must assure them an adequate level of subsistence, including housing and health care. Conceivably incentives could be devised to encourage relatives to provide family support as well. Churches and faith-based communities can play vital roles both in supporting the most vulnerable among our fellow citizens and in reinforcing the efforts of those who are conscientiously striving to develop their own capabilities.

These are ambitious proposals. They will not easily win the widespread support they require if they are to be enacted into law. Yet they may provide a model for the church's public witness. Parallel strategies can also be devised to address other problems that stem from free-market economies, especially care of the natural environment and continual vigilance to ensure the integrity of political processes. By striving for appropriate forms of government oversight of a free-market economy, we establish a framework that embraces economic processes within a more comprehensive vision of the common good.[13]

References

Anderson, Elizabeth. *Value in Ethics and Economics* (Cambridge, Mass.: Harvard University Press, 1993).

Arrow, Kenneth J. *Social Choice and Individual Values,* Second Edition (New York: Wiley, 1963).

Atkinson, A. B. *Social Justice and Public Policy* (Cambridge, Mass.: MIT Press, 1983).

Bellah, Robert N. *The Broken Covenant: American Civil Religion in a Time of Trial* (New York: Seabury Press, 1975).

Benne, Robert. *The Ethic of Democratic Capitalism: A Moral Reassessment* (Philadelphia, Penn.: Fortress Press, 1981).

Blank, Rebecca M. *Do Justice: Linking Christian Faith and Economic Life* (Cleveland, Ohio: United Church Press, 1992).

_____. *It Takes a Nation: A New Agenda for Fighting Poverty* (Princeton, N.J.: Princeton University Press, 1997).

Corrado, Anthony. *Campaign Finance Reform* (New York: The Century Foundation Press, 2000).

Daly, Herman E., and John B. Cobb. *For the Common Good: Redirecting the Economy toward Community, the Environment, and a Sustainable Future* (Boston: Beacon Press, 1994).

Elwood, David T. *The Impact of EITC and Social Reforms in Work, Marriage, and Living Arrangements* (Cambridge, Mass.: Harvard University Press, 1999).

Finn, Daniel. *Just Trading: On the Ethics and Economics of International Trade* (Nashville, Tenn.: Abingdon Press, 1996).

_____. "Global Corporate Capitalism and the Moral Ecology of Markets." *Journal of Religious Ethics* 30.1 (Winter, 2002).

Friedman, Milton. *Capitalism and Freedom* (Chicago: University of Chicago Press, 1982).

Habermas, Jürgen. *Legitimation Crisis.* Trans. Thomas McCarthy (Boston: Beacon Press, 1975).

Heilbroner, Robert, and Lester Thurow. *Economics Explained.* Newly Revised and Updated (New York: Touchstone, 1998).

Hicks, Douglas A. *Inequality and Christian Ethics* (Cambridge, England: Cambridge University Press, 2000).

Keynes, John Maynard. *The General Theory of Employment, Interest and Money* (New York: St. Martin's Press, 1973).

Krueger, David, with Donald W. Shriver and Laura L. Nash. *The Business Corporation and Productive Justice* (Nashville, Tenn.: Abingdon Press, 1997).

---

13. I wish to express my thanks to Benjamin M. Friedman, William Joseph Maier Professor of Political Economy at Harvard University, for his careful reading of an earlier draft of this paper. His observations enabled me to refine and to clarify key points in my argument.

Marx, Karl. *A Critical Analysis of Capitalist Production*, Vol. I of *Capital*. Edited by Frederick Engels, trans. Samuel Moore and Edward Aveling (New York: International Publishers, 1967).

Mooney, Christopher F. *Boundaries Dimly Perceived: Law, Religion, Education and the Common Good* (Notre Dame: Notre Dame University Press, 1989).

National Conference of Catholic Bishops. *Economic Justice for All* (Washington, D.C.: U.S. Catholic Conference, 1985).

Nordhaus, William D., and James Tobin. "Is Growth Obsolete?" In *The Measurement of Economic and Social Performance,* edited by Milton Moss (New York: National Bureau of Economic Research, Columbia University Press, 1973).

Novak, Michael. *The Spirit of Democratic Capitalism* (New York: Touchstone, 1982).

Nozick, Robert. *Anarchy, State, and Utopia* (Oxford, England: Blackwell, 1974).

Nussbaum, Martha. *Women and Human Development: The Capabilities Approach* (Cambridge, England: Cambridge University Press, 2000).

O'Connor, June. "Making a Case for the Common Good in a Global Economy: The United Nations Human Development Reports (1990–2001)." *Journal of Religious Ethics* 30.1:157–73 (2002).

Ogletree, Thomas W. "The Public Witness of the Christian Churches: Reflections Based upon Ernst Troeltsch's *Social Teaching of the Christian Churches.*" *The Annual of the Society of Christian Ethics* 1992: 43–74 (1992).

Okun, Arthur M. *Equality and Efficiency: The Big Tradeoff* (Washington, D.C.: The Brookings Institution, 1975).

Parsons, Talcott. *Politics and Social Structure* (New York: The Free Press, 1969).

Putnam, Robert D. *Bowling Alone: The Collapse and Revival of American Community* (New York: Simon & Schuster, 2000).

Rawls, John. *The Theory of Justice* (Cambridge, Mass.: Harvard University Press, 1971).

_____. *Political Liberalism* (New York: Columbia University Press, 1993).

Romano, Roberta. *The Genius of American Corporate Law* (Washington, D.C.: AEI Press, 1993).

Ryan, John A. *Economic Justice: Selections from Distributive Justice and a Living Wage.* Edited by Harlan Beckley (Louisville, Ky.: Westminster John Knox, 1996).

Schlossberg, Herbert, Vinay Samuel, and Ronald J. Sider, Eds. "The Oxford Declaration on Christian Faith and Economics," in *Christianity and Economics in the Post-Cold War Era: The Oxford Declaration and Beyond* (Grand Rapids, Mich.: William B. Eerdman's Publishing Company, 1994).

Sen, Amartya. *On Ethics and Economics*. Expanded edition (Cambridge, Mass.: Blackwell Publishers, 1988).

_____. *On Economic Inequality*. Expanded edition with an annex by James F. Foster and Amartya Sen (Oxford, England: Clarendon Press, 1997).

_____. *Development as Freedom* (New York: Alfred A. Knopf, 1999).

Sher, George. *Desert* (Princeton, N.J.: Princeton University Press, 1987).

Sider, Ronald J. *Just Generosity: A New Vision for Overcoming Poverty in America* (Grand Rapids, Mich.: Baker Books, 1999).

Smith, Adam. *An Inquiry into the Nature and Causes of the Wealth of Nations.* Reprint edited by R. H. Campbell and A. S. Skinner (Oxford, U.K.: Clarendon Press, 1776).

_____. *The Theory of Moral Sentiments.* Revised edition, reprinted 1975 (Oxford, U.K.: Clarendon Press, 1790).

Sunstein, Cass R. *Free Markets and Social Justice* (Oxford, England: Oxford University Press, 1997).

Thurow, Lester. *Generating Inequality: Mechanisms of Distribution in the U.S. Economy* (New York: Basic Books, 1975).

_____. *Zero Sum Society: Distribution and the Possibilities for Economic Change* (New York: Basic Books, 1980).

Toqueville, Alexis de. *Democracy in America*. Trans. George Lawrence. Edited by J. P. Meyer (New York: Doubleday, Anchor Books, 1969).

United Nations Development Programme. *Human Development Report* (New York: Oxford University Press, 2000).

Walzer, Michael. *Spheres of Justice. A Defense of Pluralism and Equality* (New York: Basic Books, 1983).

Weinberg, Daniel H. "A Brief Look at Postwar U.S. Income Inequality" in *Current Population Reports: Household Economic Studies* (Washington, D.C.: U.S. Census Bureau, 1996).

Wilbanks, Dana W. *Recreating America: The Ethics of U.S. Immigration and Refugee Policy in a Christian Perspective* (Nashville, Tenn.: Abingdon Press, 1996).

Wilson, William Julius. *The Truly Disadvantaged: The Inner City, the Underclass, and Public Policy* (Chicago: The University of Chicago Press, 1987).

Wogaman, Philip. *Economics and Ethics: A Christian Inquiry* (Philadelphia, Penn.: Fortress Press, 1986).

World Council of Churches. *Christian Faith and the World Economy Today* (Geneva, Switzerland: WCC Publications, 1992).

Chapter 5

Renewing Ecumenical Protestant Social Teaching

*I*n response to events surrounding civil rights demonstrations in Birmingham, Alabama, the General Board of the National Council of Churches voted in June of 1963 to establish a Commission on Religion and Race (CORR). It granted the Commission sufficient authority and funding to take strong, new initiatives in mobilizing white church participation in the civil rights struggle under the leadership of Martin Luther King Jr. The resolution calling for this step said in part:

> In such a time the Church of Jesus Christ is called upon to put aside every lesser engagement, to confess her sins of omission and delay and to move forward to witness to her essential belief that every child of God is a brother [sic] to every other. Now is the time for action—even costly action that may jeopardize the organizational goals and institutional structures of the Church, and may disrupt any fellowship that is less than fully obedient to the Lord of our Church. . . . Words and declarations are no longer useful in this struggle unless accompanied by sacrifice and commitment.[1]

The Board's action and the subsequent activities of the Commission helped to precipitate one of the most remarkable decades of clergy activism in the history of white Protestantism in America.[2] The civil rights movement furnished the impetus, the model, and the initial agenda for this activism. It introduced Protestant clergy and their progressive lay constituents to militant,

---

1. *Interchurch News* (June–July 1963) 6–7. See "NCC Acts on Racial Crisis," *Christian Century* (19 June 1963), 793. Henry J. Pratt notes that this action dramatically shifted NCC policy, from an educational strategy to public activism; *The Liberalization of American Protestantism: A Case Study in Complex Organizations* (Detroit: Wayne State University, 1972), 181–87.

2. For the work of the Commission on Religion and Race (CORR), see Anna Arnold Hedgeman, *The Trumpet Sounds: A Memoir of Negro Leadership* (New York: Halt, Rinehart & Winston, 1964); and Robert W. Spike, *The Freedom Revolution and the Churches* (New York: Association Press, 1965). On clergy

non-violent direct action as a favored means of promoting social justice in the land. While legislative action was a crucial part of the overall social aim, the proximate strategies consisted of economic pressure and political disruptions of "business as usual."

The civil rights movement peaked in 1964 and 1965 with the passage of historic new legislation requiring full access for all to public accommodations, and extending federal protections for the voting rights of citizens. Yet activist clergy were soon engaged in other social struggles: opposition to the Vietnam War, community organization among the urban poor, support for Cézar Chavez's efforts at unionizing farm workers in California, and most recently the peace movement.[3] Quite logically, the "new breed" of activist clergy also tended to support the feminist movement and the "rights" claims of non-racial minorities, in particular, persons with physical disabilities, and those with gay, lesbian, and bisexual orientations.

The Crisis in Ecumenical Protestantism

As anticipated by the Board of the National Council, this controversial social witness has in fact "jeopardized the organizational goals and institutional structures" of the ecumenical Protestant churches. The Council has been under fire for over two decades, having become a symbol of liberal social commitments which conservative constituents find objectionable. Substantial cuts in funding have resulted, forcing the Council to reduce staff and programs. CORR has long since been dismantled.[4] Protestant denominations associated with social activism have been having similar difficulties. All have experienced a steady erosion in membership, especially among young adults. Critics have attributed this trend to the ill-advised involvements of denominational leaders in social causes, perhaps to the neglect of the spiritual needs of their lay membership.[5]

---

activism, see Harvey Cox, "The 'New Breed' in American Churches: Sources of Social Activism in American Religion," in *Religion in America* (ed. Robert N. Bellah and William C. McLaughlin; Boston: Beacon, 1968), 368–83; and Harold E. Quinley, *The Prophetic Clergy: Social Activism Among Protestant Clergy* (New York: John Wiley & Sons, 1974).

3. Saul Alinsky observed: "The Churches are taking the leadership of social change." Quoted by Marion K. Sanders, "A Professional Radical Moves in on Rochester," *Harper's* (1965), 23.

4. CORR was retained until the summer of 1967, when its second director, Dr. Benjamin F. Payton, resigned to become president of Bennett College. It was reorganized as the Office of Religion and Race within the Department of Social Justice, but without the funding or the wide mandate it initially received.

5. For example, Dean M. Kelly, *Why Conservative Churches Are Growing* (New York: Harper & Row, 1977); Richard Neuhaus, *The Naked Public Square* (Grand Rapids: Eerdman's Publishing Co., 1984),

Clergy activism does appear to have caused some membership losses, especially in areas such as California where it was widespread.[6] Yet a careful analysis of the data suggests that sociodemographic factors may have played the major role in membership decline.[7] The broad generalization is that constituencies served by the ecumenical Protestant denominations have been decreasing in size in regions where these denominations historically have been strong. The salient variables include a relatively low birth rate, the postponement of marriage and childbearing by young adults, broad population shifts from the Northeast and the Midwest to the sun belt, and finally, the slowdown in the rate of "switching" from evangelical to liberal denominations. The latter shift may in part reflect relative improvements in the social standing of evangelical Protestant denominations.[8] Given factors such as these, one can project continuing membership problems for the ecumenical Protestant denominations quite apart from their stances on social questions. These denominations can reverse the pattern of membership decline only if they are able to reach new constituencies.

The primary difficulties generated by clergy activism have to do with enervating internal conflict revolving around the church's social witness. In 1969, Jeffrey Hadden detected a "gathering storm" of conflict between conservative laity and liberal clergy within the ecumenical Protestant denominations.[9] The storm has since broken. It has not been so furious as a hurricane nor so intense as a tornado, but " 't is enough, 't will do." Conservative lay members now display less confidence in denominational structures, and less willingness to grant allegiance to denominational programs. Financial support has dropped, though not so sharply as the fall in membership. Conservative factions have

233–36; Peter L. Berger, "American Religion: Conservative Upsurge, Liberal Prospects," in *Liberal Protestantism: Realities and Possibilities* (ed. Robert S. Michaelson and Wade Clark Roof; New York: Pilgrim, 1986), 24–28, 33–36.

6. Quinley, *The Prophetic Clergy*.

7. William McKinney and Wade Clark Roof, "Liberal Protestantism: A Sociodemographic Perspective," in *Liberal Protestantism*, 37–50.

8. The birth rate in ecumenical Protestant denominations is 1.97, compared with 2.54 in conservative Protestant denominations. 2.1 is required for replacement. Even a birth rate of 2.25, the national average, would have meant an increase of a million members in ecumenical Protestant denominations (McKinney and Roof, "Liberal Protestantism," 43–44). Ecumenical Protestant denominations continue to benefit from "switching," with a net gain of 1.9 percent in exchanges with other groups (ibid., 45–47). Yet the rate of switching from conservative to ecumenical Protestant denominations is down from previous decades (William R Hutchinson, "Past Imperfect: History and the Prospect for Liberalism," in *Liberal Protestantism*, 68–69). Most ecumenical Protestant losses are not to other denominations but to nonaffiliation. They are most serious among young adults (McKinney and Roof, "Liberal Protestantism," 46–47). The loss of young adults may be related to the recent trend toward postponing marriage and child-bearing.

9. Jeffrey K. Hadden, *The Gathering Storm in the Churches* (Garden City, NY: Doubleday, 1969).

formed independent agencies which reflect their own vision of the church's mission. These agencies compete for resources with official denominational structures. In response to lay objections, ecumenical denominations have moderated their social witness, giving fresh emphasis to traditional concerns for evangelism and personal spiritual growth. Many activist clergy have become disillusioned. Not a few have left the ministry altogether. Others have had difficulty in securing suitable positions to continue their ministries.[10] Such complex internal struggles do not make for a confident, cohesive ministry. They signal a church in trouble. Above all they place in doubt the capacities of ecumenical Protestant denominations to sustain an activist social witness.

The Roots of Internal Conflict

In retrospect, the divisive conflicts within ecumenical Protestantism appear altogether predictable on both sociological and historical grounds. Hadden has highlighted the sociological factors. The underlying problem is that most lay members of the ecumenical Protestant denominations are socially conservative. Yet they have been pressed by clergy leaders to honor, if not support, vigorous efforts to bring about social change. Given their social locations, they have not been disposed to identify with the social vision which informs these efforts. Still less have they been prepared to accept as valid the militancy and political partisanship of activist clergy.[11] Clergy in the ecumenical Protestant denominations came from the same social backgrounds as their lay membership. Yet in their formation as ministers they were exposed to experiences which sensitized them to urban poverty, racial injustice, the subordination of women, and the oppression suffered by millions of people in the "third world." They learned to integrate a sense of accountability for such suffering with their basic grasp of the Gospel.

The sociological bases of internal Protestant conflict have been widely discussed. We have not, however, paid sufficient attention to the historical factors. My thesis is that the recent social witness of the Protestant churches, epitomized in the public involvements of clergy activists, went considerably beyond—and in some respects counter to—well-founded traditions of social thought in American Christianity. In this respect they cut across deep, taken-for-granted beliefs about the meaning of being Christian in America. I hasten

10. Quinley, *The Prophetic Clergy.*
11. See ibid., 7–11, 159–84, 298–99.

to state my convictions that the recent Protestant social witness did have solid biblical and theological bases.[12] I believe it also had important precedents in American history in the activities of socially concerned Christians. At the same time, the understandings upon which this witness rested had never been deeply assimilated within white Protestantism. We can examine this claim with reference to the central themes of the ecumenical Protestant witness: concern for racial justice, advocacy for the poor, resistance to an unjust war, and opposition to the nuclear arms race. In regard to none of these matters is there a widely recognized moral heritage within popular American Christianity.

To be specific, white Protestantism as a whole had never displayed deep concern for racial equality and inclusiveness. Some white Protestant denominations did initially condemn slavery, and there were pockets of abolitionist activity by white Protestants in the nineteenth century. Further, the northern branches of white Protestant denominations did eventually unite in opposition to slavery. Following emancipation, however, they more or less joined their southern counterparts in expecting freed African Americans to assume subordinate roles in the society. They presumed the essential superiority of the "Anglo-Saxon" race. Following the period of reconstruction, they accepted segregation as an appropriate structure for race relations.[13] Even spokespersons for the social gospel had little to say about race, emphasizing instead the primacy of economic issues.[14] Only gradually and with caution did the Protestant churches move toward a stronger advocacy of racial justice. When white Protestant leaders decided to become an active part of the civil rights movement, they broke sharply with prevailing racial attitudes in their churches.

Similarly, the Protestant churches, whether Black or white, characteristically supported American wars. African American churches took this stand in part to demonstrate to the white majority that their members were loyal citizens.[15] White Protestants supported American wars more out of a basic confidence in America's positive role in God's purposes for the world. They viewed the various wars as means of extending the civilizing mission of the Christian churches.[16] Clergy activists of the sixties, most notably Dr. Martin Luther King Jr., took a fateful new step when they challenged the justice of

12. See Thomas W. Ogletree, *The Use of the Bible in Christian Ethics* (Philadelphia: Fortress, 1983).

13. See Robert T. Handy, *A Christian America: Protestant Hopes and Historical Realities* (2d ed., revised and enlarged; New York: Oxford University, 1984), 105–10.

14. Ibid., 178–81.

15. John H. Cartwright, "The Black Church and the Call for Peace," *The Drew Gateway* 54 (Fall 1983), 55.

16. See Handy, *A Christian America,* 124–27.

America's involvement in Vietnam.[17] Having exposed the illegitimacy of that war, they became increasingly critical of governmental definitions of the security interests of the nation. They were ready to oppose the nuclear arms race and any further military interventions in the internal affairs of other peoples. In view of the strong traditions of Protestant support for American wars, it is hardly surprising that their opposition to the Vietnam war and support for a nuclear freeze appeared to many to reflect disloyalty to the nation.

The concern for urban poverty grew out of the civil rights movement as African American leaders recognized with increasing sharpness that guarantees of civil rights and rights of access to public accommodations could not touch the economic sources of Black suffering. The proximate response was a commitment to the empowerment of the poor through community organization, the mobilization of welfare recipients, and support for action-oriented community groups. For a time federal legislation, enacted as part of Lyndon Johnson's "war on poverty," provided legitimacy and funding for these efforts. White Protestant churches became involved in the empowerment of the poor through ecumenical consortia and through the direct participation of individual congregations. Federal support for community-action programs was phased out when it became apparent that they were generating problems for local authorities. The churches were, however, implicated in the controversies surrounding these actions.

The social gospel furnished precedents for Christian concern about economic injustices. Yet here, too, the initiatives of the sixties represented a new turn in Protestant teaching. The social gospel had primarily addressed the interests of workers in the new industrial order. It took for granted the capacity of modern industry to generate sufficient wealth, under acceptable conditions of production, to provide for the well-being of all. It did not confront anything comparable to more contemporary urban realities, which amount to a systemic abandonment of substantial segments of the population to chronic poverty, where crime and drugs and prostitution are the chief means of survival. Racism figures strongly in the present public acceptance of the degradation of the poor. By relating to community action projects among the urban poor, churches and pastors came up against complex structural barriers to human hopes of escaping poverty. These barriers drove them to a more critical look at basic American institutions than had been typical of the social gospel.

Clergy activists not only represented a substantive social witness which

17. Martin Luther King Jr., "A Prophecy for the '80's: Martin Luther King, Jr.'s 'Beyond Vietnam' Speech," *Sojourners* (January 1983); Cartwright, "The Black Church," 56–58. See also Martin Luther King Jr., "A Christmas Sermon on Peace," *Trumpet of Conscience* (New York: Harper & Row, 1967).

outran established traditions of Protestant social teaching. In taking up King's model of militant non-violent direct action, they also utilized methods which were alien to those traditions. American Protestant teaching had been essentially voluntarist in orientation. In matters of conscience it emphasized persuasion and resisted suggestions of coercion. The voluntary spirit grew out of ideas of religious freedom; but its origins lay in the evangelical understanding of salvation, where the human capacity to refuse even God's offer of saving grace is explicitly recognized. Within evangelical Protestantism freedom has meant freedom of choice.

American Protestants were not always consistent in their voluntarism.[18] They fought for the prohibition amendment and for legislation to protect the Christian "sabbath." They called for mandatory attendance at public schools, which functioned as Protestant schools. They sought to embody their sexual codes in public law, and they advocated or at least accepted legal segregation.[19] They viewed these matters as requisites of social order, or more specifically, as the necessary social conditions of an effective evangelical witness. On other concerns, however, Protestants usually stressed voluntarism, moral suasion, appeals to conscience and goodwill. They moved reluctantly to legislative solutions to social problems. Wherever possible they avoided coercive strategies, such as strikes, boycotts, or mass demonstrations.

Both King and the people who adopted his style of social witness retained the voluntary spirit of Protestant Christianity. But they combined moral suasion with socially disruptive tactics. In so doing, they generated a power base from which to negotiate new social policies, albeit within the framework of the existing social order. By following such tactics, clergy activists departed from accepted notions of proper ministerial roles.

The Quest for Christian America

Robert Handy's study, *A Christian America* (1984), suggests that the historical sources of conflict within American Protestantism are deeper and more pervasive than simply a number of disputes on selected social issues. His thesis is that American Protestants have from our colonial beginnings been driven by a dream of a Christian America. This dream was present in the Puritan and Anglican traditions of the earliest colonies. Especially strong was the Calvinist sense of the responsibility of the elect to promote the public good.

18. Handy, *A Christian America,* 54–58.
19. Ibid., 85–94, 101–5.

The dream of Christian America continued unabated after the adoption of the First Amendment to the Constitution, which barred any establishment of religion. However, the institutional base of this dream was no longer an established church, but rather voluntary churches, or better, Protestant denominations.[20] The denomination, I would suggest, is an adaptation of the "church type" of ecclesiastical organization (Troeltsch) to a situation where establishment is precluded. It is voluntary in its formal constitution, yet it is so fully integrated with the basic institutions of society that it takes on the sociocultural functions of an established church. Thus, the denominations in their plurality became variant modalities of an overarching Protestant establishment.

The rapidly growing evangelical denominations—Methodist, Baptist, and later, Disciples of Christ—soon surpassed in size and influence the older Anglican and Reformed communions. Yet they readily appropriated the latter's assumptions about the Christian substance of civilization. They reconceived the Puritan sense of the public responsibility of the elect as the public responsibility of the converted. Protestant denominations competed with each other for members, and they intensely debated key theological questions. Yet to a remarkable degree, they agreed about Christian America. They believed that America "worked" because its people and its institutions were pervasively Christian.

The vision of Christian America bore with it the conviction that America had a peculiar role in human history. America, our forebears believed, was God's new instrument for the redemption of the world. This sense of national destiny energized the churches in their evangelistic mission. It was a powerful factor in their extraordinary commitment of resources to world missions. It gave church leaders confidence that even the secularists would recognize the social contributions of the churches and support the conditions of their flourishing. By the late nineteenth century, Handy notes,[21] the focus of the church's mission had almost become its civilizing role in the world. Protestant leaders contended that America had absorbed much of the spirit of Christianity. It was charged with disseminating that spirit to the world through its global reach. Thus, the Protestant social witness of the sixties—dealing with issues of race, poverty, and America's geopolitical involvements—did not simply go beyond well-established precedents in Protestant social teaching. In each case it placed in question Protestant presumptions of America's basic goodness and of her liberating, enlightening role in world history.

King's own pilgrimage is illuminating here. King began his labors with a

20. Ibid., 42–54.
21. Ibid., 95.

sense of congruence between the Christian vision of freedom and the American dream of liberty. He believed that the civil rights movement was firmly grounded in both. As he grew in his awareness of the deep interpenetration of racism with the desperate circumstances of the poor, he saw more clearly the dubious underside of basic American institutions. His increased unease with America was reinforced when he reflected on the significance of U.S. involvement in the Vietnam war, including the links between that involvement and the suffering of Black Americans.[22] The Protestant confidence in America's civilizing role in the world had begun to erode.[23]

Because of the sharpness of their critique of America during the sixties and seventies, ecumenical Protestant leaders and the denominations they served were less able to draw nourishment for their activities from the patriotic sensibilities of the American people. Nor were they as likely to benefit from the world-transforming impact of American economic and military might. Here as well the ecumenical Protestant social witness has come into conflict with historical Protestant convictions about America's place in God's purposes for the world. Patriotism has by no means lost all legitimacy within a Protestant social witness, nor has it become improper to celebrate the social and political accomplishments of the American people. There is much to affirm about America, provided the affirmation is also critical. Even so, ecumenical Protestant social teaching can no longer be intimately tied to hopes for a Christian America. These hopes have ceased to have a basis in reality. Indeed, given the religious diversity of the nation, they have lost their moral legitimacy as well. Churches must give up these ideas and learn to do their work without the support they once provided.

The Resurgent Evangelical Witness of the "Christian Right"

As the ecumenical Protestant social witness generated increasing conflicts within "mainline" Protestantism, a new "Christian Right" began to emerge that largely reclaimed the nineteenth-century evangelical/populist vision for a Christian America. Utilizing public media, Jerry Falwell and Pat Robertson were initially the most publicly visible leaders of this movement, though many other actors have played crucial roles as well. As a social and political

---

22. James H. Cone, "Martin Luther King, Jr., Black Theology, and the Black Church," *The Drew Gateway* 56 (Winter 1985), 1–17.
23. See Joseph C. Hough Jr., "The Loss of Optimism as a Problem for Liberal Christian Faith," in *Liberal Protestantism: Realities and Possibilities* (ed. Robert S. Michaelson and Wade Clark Roof; New York: Pilgrim, 1986), 145–66.

movement, the new Christian Right has achieved impressive clarity and focus, and it has employed strategies for promoting its message that are likely to play some role in virtually any effective public witness by Christian churches in a liberal, democratic society.

The message of the Christian Right has centered upon traditional "family values," embracing patriarchal authority, mothers remaining in the household, and strict discipline in the nurture of children. These values have been judged to be at grave risk because of secularizing trends in American life and culture. In advancing its message, the Christian Right has appealed to Scripture, to long-standing American practices, and to plain "common sense."[24] In conjunction with its commitment to family values, it has aggressively opposed divorce, abortions, homosexual practices, and pornography. Opposition to abortion has also encompassed attempts to block stem cell research, even though such research could potentially generate cures for genetically transmitted diseases. Stem cell research is opposed because the cells utilized in such research are associated either with abortions or with medical practices designed to enable childless couples to have children of their own.

On these particular issues, there is striking congruence between official Roman Catholic teachings and the message of the Christian Right. Pope John Paul II has succinctly addressed these matters in his encyclical, *Evangelium Vitae,* or "The Gospel of Life" (1995).[25] The encyclical focuses on "crimes against life" that have gradually become socially acceptable, in some instances with the full complicity of modern health-care systems! The pope condemns all acts of murder as "intrinsically evil," but he focuses attention on abortion as a contemporary instance of murder. Though he acknowledges that artificial contraceptives may in some cases eliminate a subsequent temptation to abortion, his primary interest is to dramatize the close connection that holds between contraception and abortion. In contrast to "responsible parenthood" the "contraceptive mentality" actually strengthens the tempta-

24. See Robert C. Lieman and Robert Wuthnow, eds., *The New Christian Right* (New York: Praeger Publishers, 1983); Grant Wacker, "Speaking of Norman Rockwell: Popular Evangelicalism in Contemporary America," in Leonard Sweet, ed., *The Evangelical Tradition in America* (Macon, GA: Mercer University Press, 1992); and Duane Murray Oldfield, *The Right and the Righteous: The Christian Right Confronts the Republican Party* (New York: Rowman & Littlefield Publishers, Inc., 1996). Richard Viguerie and Howard Phillips were cofounders of the Conservative Caucus. Paul Weyrich and Wedwin Fuelner formed the Heritage Foundation. Senator Jesse Helms and Terry Dolan of the National Conservative Political Action Committee (NCPAC) declared themselves "New Right" leaders (Oldfield, 96). They advocated militant anti-Communism and anti-unionism, and opposed big government. They also denounced abortion rights, feminism, and pornography.

25. The encyclical *Evangelium Vitae* was delivered by Pope John Paul II on March 25, 1995. See Joseph G. Doners, ed., *John Paul II: The Encyclicals in Everyday Language* (Maryknoll, NY: Orbis Books, 1996), 242–90.

tion to abortion should an unwanted life be conceived. The pope specifically mentions the use of "effective pharmaceuticals to kill the fetus in the mother's womb without recourse to medical assistance," a reference to what is commonly known as the "morning after" pill. He challenges the "hedonistic mentality" that refuses to accept responsibility in matters of sexuality, a mentality that regards procreation as an obstacle to personal self-fulfillment. He is equally critical of techniques of "artificial reproduction" because they separate procreation from the "fully human context of the conjugal act." Not only do these techniques have a high rate of failure, they produce a surplus of embryos as well. These embryos are then either destroyed or used for medical research, reducing human life to mere "biological material." The pope also raises questions about "prenatal diagnosis." This process can in principle be morally justified provided it is directed toward medical treatments for a child in the womb. The problem is that prenatal diagnosis can lead to "eugenic" abortions that cannot be justified. The crucial point is that abortion, and all medical practices directly or indirectly associated with abortion, are intrinsically evil acts. What is noteworthy for Protestants, moreover, is that the pope elaborates the "Gospel of Life" not by appeals to principles of natural law but by an eloquent recitation of basic biblical and theological teachings about God's gracious bestowal of life in creating and sustaining the universe. In this respect as well, his message is congruent with the witness of the Christian Right.[26]

The "family values" agenda of the Christian Right embraces an insistence upon the "free exercise of religion" in the public contexts of American life: prayer in public schools, public displays of Christian symbols on town greens or in urban centers, the inclusion of "creation science" in public school curricula along with secular theories of evolution, and more generally, the restoration of "Judeo-Christian values" in educational institutions. The family focus was later expanded to encompass local control of public education, school vouchers and school choice, parental rights in overseeing school policies, and tax breaks and welfare changes to benefit families that "stay together."

Finally, Pat Robertson has stressed America's providential role in world affairs. He has called into question the rapid development of strong international institutions, both political and economic. Such institutions, he contends,

---

26. What distinguishes "The Gospel of Life" from the message of the Christian Right is that Pope John Paul II explicitly links concerns about abortion and euthanasia to a broad array of concerns about life: (1) violence and hatred that lead to war, slaughter, and genocide; (2) human beings, especially children, forced into poverty, malnutrition, and hunger because of the "unjust distribution of resources"; and (3) the scandalous arms trade, the "reckless tampering with the world's ecological balance," and the spread of drugs. Nonetheless, abortion remains the predominant theme in the encyclical's discussion of "intrinsic evils."

will subvert national sovereignty, and they will open the way for the global manipulation of financial markets to the disadvantage of the American people.[27] From the time of its founding, he argues, America has been "God's chosen people," a people called to advance God's purposes for the world. In Robertson's view, the fulfillment of this mission requires national sovereignty, a strong national defense, an aggressive anticommunist crusade, and support for the state of Israel. The Christian Right has consistently supported the goals and objectives of the state of Israel, including its more expansive "Zionist" visions. In more general terms, Robertson has called upon the American people to renounce secularism and to revitalize their Judeo-Christian heritage.[28] Thus, in the context of the Cold War, the Christian Right essentially reclaimed the nineteenth-century Protestant dream of a Christian American. In effect, it exposed the betrayal of this dream by ecumenical Protestant leaders who opposed the Vietnam War, who resisted President Reagan's commitment to the nuclear arms race, and who expressly supported international organizations and agencies designed to foster peace and global cooperation in a conflict-ridden world.

The Christian Right has been equally impressive in developing a range of independent organizations both to communicate its message and to devise effective political strategies for implementing that message in public law and in public policies. These organizations have been self-consciously designed to appeal to evangelical Protestant constituencies. At the same time, their operations have remained independent of any direct oversight by local congregations and denominational bodies. This independence has enabled them to focus their energies on an explicitly political agenda, and it has allowed evangelical churches to preserve the integrity of their own spiritual missions. The National Christian Action Coalition, founded in 1978, was the first of these new organizations. It was followed by the Religious Roundtable, the Christian Voice, the Moral Majority, Concerned Women for America, the Freedom Council, and the American Coalition for Traditional Values, and the list has continued to grow.

Under the leadership of Ralph Reed, the Christian Coalition, organized by Pat Robertson, became the foremost political action organization of the Christian Right. Reed served as executive director of the Coalition from its found-

---

27. Cf. Pat Robertson, *The New World Order* (Dallas: Word Publishing, 1991). Robertson specifically criticized the so-called Trilateral Commission, headed by David Rockefeller and Zbigniew Brezinski, which was seeking to strengthen working relationships between Japan, Europe, and the United States. Robertson charged the commission with organizing a "three-cornered world system" to "manage the world economy" and to pave the way for "world government." Cf. Robertson, 102.

28. Cf. Robertson, *America's Dates with Destiny* (Nashville: Thomas Nelson Publishers, 1986).

ing in 1989 until 1997. By 1995, the Christian Coalition had 1.6 million members with 1,600 local chapters and $25 million in funds.[29] To advance its political agenda, the Christian Coalition built collaborative links with the Republican Party. This strategy inescapably involved compromises, that is, support for candidates and for legislative priorities that did not fully exemplify the message of the Christian Right but that at least embodied incremental steps toward the realization of some of its larger goals. Representative examples include legislation to outlaw "partial birth" abortions and legislation that explicitly holds a person accountable for the death of an unborn child should that person be charged with killing a pregnant woman. What had once been a single murder has now become a double murder. The effect of such legislation is to reinforce broader claims about the right to life of a fetus from the moment of conception. More recently, the Christian Right has mobilized support for an amendment to the U.S. Constitution that would define marriage as a union between a man and a woman. Though such an amendment appears unlikely to succeed, it keeps public attention focused on a major item in the public agenda of the Christian Right.

The Christian Right has impacted ecumenical Protestantism in a number of ways. To begin with there are substantial constituencies in ecumenical Protestant denominations who share at least some of the beliefs advocated by the Christian Right, particularly in regard to abortion, homosexuality, and pornography. In many instances, these constituencies have formed independent organizations of their own to counter the influence of official denominational and ecumenical agencies. An example would be the "Confessing Movement" within United Methodism, or the Institute for Religion and Democracy, whose activities are manifest in most of the major ecumenical Protestant denominations. Evangelical criticisms of secularizing trends in ecumenical Protestant denominations have undoubtedly played a role as well in reducing earlier patterns of membership shifts from evangelical to "mainline" churches. These shifts had been primarily associated with advancements in social status, not simply changes in religious beliefs. In recent decades, evangelical Protestantism has itself gained increased social standing in American life, rendering irrelevant earlier patterns of membership changes. Likewise, the high public profile of the Christian Right has indirectly reduced the levels of access to public officials that leaders of

---

29. Cf. The Christian Coalition, *Contract with the American Family* (Nashville: Moorings, 1995). See also Ralph Reed, *Active Faith: How Christians Are Changing the Soul of American Politics* (New York: The Free Press, 1996), and Justin Watson, *The Christian Coalition: Dreams of Restoration, Demands for Recognition* (New York: St. Martin's Press, 1997).

ecumenical Protestant churches traditionally enjoyed, complicating their efforts to exercise a public voice.

At a more fundamental level, efforts by the Christian Right and by Roman Catholic officials to promote a "public morals" agenda have provoked attempts by civil libertarians, for example, the American Civil Liberties Union (ACLU), to challenge the legitimacy of any efforts by faith-based organizations to promote their public causes on distinctively religious grounds. Civil libertarians insist that the wall separating church and state must remain impenetrable. Philosophers specializing in public ethics have added their own voices to this debate, calling for public discourse that is restricted to publicly redeemable claims. John Rawls has characterized this narrowed focus as a "thin" theory of the good, one specifically limited to the political spheres of society.[30] These libertarian claims cannot be casually dismissed. They are driven by resolute commitments to resist any possible encroachment on the disestablishment clause in the First Amendment to the Constitution. They are flawed, however, because of their failure to make clear distinctions between two forms of religious expression in public discourse: on the one hand, discourse advocating particular forms of public morals legislation; and on the other, discourse focusing on laws and policies that promise to enhance the common good of the society, insofar as government can play a role in fostering that good. In a liberal democracy, discourse of the former sort is inherently problematic insofar as it seeks the enactment of coercive laws that will enforce personal moral standards in the private lives of free individuals, even though the underlying grounds for those standards are derived from the authoritative traditions of particular religious communities. In contrast, debates about the proper role of government in advancing the common good can frequently be enriched by prophetic visions of human well being, even when those visions explicitly draw upon the accumulated wisdom of discrete religious traditions.

Though the public morals agenda usually collides with principles of liberal democracy, it still merits a respectful hearing because it raises questions that

---

30. The list of relevant works is enormous, but the works of John Rawls and Jürgen Habermas have been especially compelling. See Rawls's final monograph on the issues, *Justice as Fairness: A Restatement* (Cambridge, MA: Harvard University Press, 2001); and Habermas's *Moral Consciousness and Communicative Action*, trans. by C. Lenhardt and S. W. Nicholsen (Cambridge, MA: MIT Press, 1993). Thomas McCarthy effectively relates the work of these two scholars to the legacy of Immanuel Kant in "Kantian Constructivism and Reconstructivism: Rawls and Habermas in Dialogue," *Ethics* 105 (October 1994). Ronald F. Thiemann provides a balanced overview of the issues in *Religion and Public Life: A Dilemma for Democracy* (Washington, D.C.: Georgetown University Press, 1996). See also Robert Audi and Nicholas Wolterstorff, *Religion in the Public Square: The Place of Religious Conviction in Political Debate* (Lanham, MD: Rowman and Littlefield Publishers, 1997).

can prove to be highly important for the well-being of human societies. Ecumenical Protestants, for example, normally do not view abortion as a good thing, not even when they insist upon a woman's right to "procreative choice." Their primary interest is to prevent unwanted pregnancies in order to reduce dramatically the need for an abortion in the first place. Furthermore, an embryo or a fetus is certainly a form of human life, albeit at a primitive stage of development. By itself, however, this primal fact does not warrant the conclusion that a fetus in the early weeks of pregnancy already possesses the same rights to life as a fully formed person. Still less does it bestow upon the state the authority to override a woman's right of control over her own bodily functions in order to assure the survival of the fetus at any cost. Equally important, though abortions are hardly the optimal strategy for dealing with unwanted pregnancies, their legal availability still merits support for concrete, practical reasons. When laws prohibiting abortions under all circumstances were rigorously enforced, their impact fell primarily upon the most vulnerable women in society—women who had been subjected to sexual abuse or women in poverty who had few options for coping with an unwanted pregnancy. Women who were more affluent could, after all, simply fly to Canada to secure a safe, legal abortion. They would in any case have ample resources for child care. Prior to Roe v. Wade, emergency rooms in urban hospitals frequently received women patients, often teenagers, who were on the verge of bleeding to death because of a perforated uterus. This condition resulted from illegal abortions performed by persons without medical training. Since Roe v. Wade, such cases have virtually disappeared from hospital emergency rooms precisely because all women now have access to safe, legal abortions.[31] Finally, it should be recognized that ecumenical Protestants have hardly been advocates of promiscuous sex. They have supported the public distribution of contraceptive devices essentially as a realistic strategy aimed at curbing both unwanted pregnancies and sexually transmitted diseases, in particular, HIV/AIDS. A pro-life agenda that simply disregards these facts is hardly facing up to the challenges of affirming human life in the midst of a sinful and fallen world.

Contemporary debates about same-sex marriages present slightly different challenges because they involve overlapping private and public dimensions. In important respects, marriage is a sacral institution, one deeply rooted in formative faith traditions. Consequently, faith-based communities

---

31. I was informed of this dramatic shift in the world of hospital emergency rooms while participating in an interdisciplinary course on medical ethics at the Vanderbilt University Medical School during the mid-seventies.

must themselves determine (1) whether they should authorize marriage rites for same-sex couples; (2) whether they should openly acknowledge and also honor couples within their own membership who are living in same-sex civil unions or partnerships; and (3) whether they should allow persons living in same-sex marriages, civil unions, or partnerships to be ordained or to exercise lay leadership in faith-based communities. In most churches, these issues are highly controversial, and these controversies will not be resolved quickly. Yet debates about same-sex marriages also involve questions of civil rights and public law, especially since a substantial number of legal benefits at both state and federal levels are associated with the institution of marriage. The public dimensions of the debates about same-sex marriage essentially involve questions about human rights, that is, whether persons who identify themselves as gay, lesbian, or bisexual are entitled to the same rights as those that are guaranteed for all other members of the society. Thus, even faith-based communities that consider homosexual practices to be incompatible with their own teachings are still obliged to honor the full human rights of all persons regardless of their specific beliefs regarding homosexuality or the appropriateness of homosexual practices and relationships. So far as I can see, there is no compelling counterpart to this latter claim. Not only is a Constitutional amendment defining marriage as a union between a man and a woman unlikely to pass, it is even more certain that such an amendment, if passed, could not withstand rigorous judicial scrutiny. In public life, in other words, debates about same-sex marriages finally boil down to debates about basic human rights.

Within the context of a liberal democracy it is inappropriate on both Constitutional and ethical grounds for faith-based communities and organizations to press for the enactment of coercive public laws whose purpose is to enforce moral standards that are essentially personal in nature, especially when the moral authority that underlies those standards largely derives from the distinctive traditions of discrete religious communities. Given the importance of sustaining Constitutional principles of limited government, principles that preserve basic human liberties against illegitimate government intrusion, personal moral standards can best be promoted in the private sector. Exceptions to this principle must be restricted to cases that either violate the private interests of other persons and groups or manifestly place in jeopardy vital public interests. Public pornographic displays violate the sensibilities of persons who consider those displays offensive, and illegal, highly addictive drugs endanger both public health and social order. Action in the private sector is in no case restricted to purely individual choices. It embraces as well the collective initiatives of voluntary associations and organizations, including churches, that are composed of persons who freely exercise their own conscientious judgments.

The Protestant Social Witness in a Post-Christian America

How shall we renew ecumenical Protestant social teaching in a post-Christian America? Here I can only outline a basic approach, highlighting the nurture of congregations and suggesting priorities that should guide efforts to cultivate an authentically Christian social witness.

1. Equipping Congregations for a Social Witness

While a Christian social vision may be compatible with the greater American ethos, it will inevitably have points of strain with that ethos. It will at least have emphases, nuances, and priorities that are not readily valued within the society as a whole, especially for centers of power that tend to dominate social policy. Consequently, there can be no effective ecumenical Protestant social witness without healthy congregations capable of nurturing and sustaining such a witness. This point holds even for societies that have an established church. It has special pertinence for the post-Christian society that has taken form in contemporary America.[32]

Unlike our predecessors, we can no longer take the church for granted, nor can we presume to speak directly to public issues out of a Christian perspective. Both tendencies are holdovers from the informal Protestant establishment of earlier decades. Because a Christian witness requires a discrete social-communal base, Christian social ethics inescapably involves congregational development.

Congregations are essentially religious communities. They derive their power from faith in the triune God: creator and sustainer of the universe, redemptive presence in Jesus Christ, and renewing power in human life through the presence of the Holy Spirit. Churches can never be mere instruments of social change. They may be one of God's means for the redemption of the world; but they serve best as means when they are also ends in themselves, concrete communities that embody in their own life practices the saving promises of the Gospel. The post-World War II affirmation of the ecumenical churches is sound: the first task of the church is to be the church. This affirmation means

---

32. See chapter 2, "The Public Witness of the Christian Churches," especially the references to Ernst Troeltsch, *The Social Teaching of the Christian Churches* (Louisville, KY: Westminster John Knox Press, 1992), 1006–7.

that the social witness of the church must be of a piece with its spirituality, with its activities in nurturing faith, and with the character of its internal fellowship. Only if these latter elements are present can the church foster a distinctively Christian social vision among those who share its common life. Such a vision presupposes the possibility of awakening in human beings moral commitments that go beyond interests associated with their specific social locations.

An expansion of social vision cannot be achieved simply through conventional educational programs or authoritative proclamations from the pulpit, though both are relevant. It is possible only if congregations, or at least influential groups within a congregation, have significant experiences with fellow human beings who are differently situated in the social world, persons whose perceptions open up dimensions of understanding that are not otherwise readily available to most church members. Insofar as the churches remain nothing more than homogenous social enclaves, they will be unable to grasp the radical notions of inclusiveness or of solidarity with the poor and the marginal that are so central to the Gospel message. Denominational and ecumenical structures are crucial to the social witness of the churches. They enable local congregations to overcome their parochialism and social homogeneity by linking them to multiple facets of the church's mission, including its global connections. Indeed, the church's global reach has gained increasing urgency in a world that is substantially molded by the economic priorities of powerful multinational corporations and by the prevailing interests of international political and economic organizations. The World Council of Churches fosters an appreciation for multicultural understandings, understandings that can counter hegemonic tendencies in policies administered by the United Nations Security Council, the International Monetary Fund, the World Bank, or the World Trade Organization.

2. The Public Witness of the Churches

While the first task of the church is to be the church, being the church includes public responsibility—a world calling—especially in the United States where faithful Christians are in a position to contribute to the well-being of society as a whole. The motivation for taking up such responsibility can no longer derive, however, from the expectation that America can be transformed into a Christian nation. Nor can it stem from the conviction that America is God's special instrument for the redemption of the world.[33] Protestant churches have a public role in American society because Protestant Christians have genuine,

---

33. Cf. Harold Hongju Koh, "On American Exceptionalism," *Stanford Law Review* 55 (May, 2003), 1479–1527.

albeit limited, power and influence within the society. They are accountable to God and to one another, therefore, for the ways in which they exercise their public responsibilities.

I would highlight four matters that are crucial to the renewal of a viable ecumenical Protestant social witness in contemporary American society. First, the church's social witness must primarily address public conditions that are requisite to the common social good. This focus stands in contrast to the "public morals agenda" of the Christian Right. Second, the church's social witness must include attempts to foster more constructive working relationships with diverse religious bodies, demonstrating that a faith-based voice in a democratic society need not be divisive, that it can actually enhance broader social bonds. Third, a Christian social witness requires a coherent and substantive account of distinctively Christian social teachings, one that is relevant to the formative values and operative organizational principles of a particular society. Finally, a Christian social witness requires independent action-oriented organizations that are capable of mobilizing public support for specific political objectives. As in the case of the Christian Right, organizations of this sort are most effective when they remain largely independent of the ongoing faith practices of congregations and denominational bodies.

The proper focus of ecumenical Protestant social teaching is the common social good of a religiously and culturally diverse society, not some attempt to access public resources in order to advance particular church interests. In principle this good extends to the ends of the inhabited earth, insofar as the policies and practices of a given society play a role in that larger arena. Within a liberal democracy, the common good cannot be associated with some comprehensive vision of how human beings can best achieve personal and collective fulfillment in an ideal world. It is rather about ordering basic social, economic, and political institutions in ways that sustain conditions under which all members of society are able to develop their capabilities and to exercise their basic freedoms as persons of dignity and worth. This orientation primarily concerns the proper role of government in human affairs. In practical terms, therefore, debates about the common good embrace Constitutional issues, public legislation, and critical assessments of policies managed by governmental departments and agencies at federal, state, and local levels. These matters are far reaching in their import, and they impact most facets of human life, directly or indirectly. Of special importance are laws and policies that facilitate and also provide oversight for a free market economy, and programs that provide vitally important social services.

Government oversight of the economy embraces matters such as monetary policy; corporate law; the regulation of trade, commerce, and stock exchanges;

protections for consumers against unsafe products and unreliable services; and laws and policies that place constraints on social practices that endanger the natural environment.[34] The range of public services delivered by federal, state, and local governments is equally broad. These services include the maintenance of public order and national security; the sustenance of stable international relationships, including collaborative participation in international organizations and agencies; protections for human and civil liberties; and provisions for transportation facilities, basic utilities, public education, safeguards for public health, unemployment benefits, and social security. In modern society, public policy issues are unavoidably complex, requiring a broad range of technical competencies, embracing such matters as public law, jurisprudence, economics, international relations, public administration, policy studies, engineering, and human science perspectives on the requisites of human development. For the most part, competencies such as these fall outside of distinctively religious perspectives. Nonetheless, they provide practical knowledge that is itself quite indispensable for constructive engagements with public policy issues. In this regard a Christian social witness does require "think tanks" capable of generating the requisite expertise in particular facets of public life.

Public debates invariably involve ideological disputes as well, that is, political philosophies that legitimate particular sets of policy priorities, often in ways that serve special interests at the expense of a broader public good. Indeed, party politics typically center on ideological disputes that reflect competing centers of power within the society, effectively pushing aside candid debates about how best to foster a broader public good. These ideological disputes can themselves become "discussion stoppers" when advocates of adversarial positions simply refuse to subject their respective claims to open and discursive criticism. The central point is that effective political action invariably involves power struggles of some sort. This reality accounts for the fact that a distinctively Christian social witness necessarily involves independent organizations capable of mobilizing support for particular public causes. In no case, however, can the political process legitimately disregard critical considerations of the proper role of government in fostering social conditions essential to human flourishing. The "family values" agenda of the Christian Right and the pro-life agenda of Roman Catholic officials have both tended to overstep boundaries that constrain government actions in a liberal democracy. The principle of limited government entails the vigorous protection of substantial space for private initiatives by free persons and the free associa-

---

34. See chapter 4, "Corporate Capitalism and the Common Good."

tions to which they freely belong. Faith-based communities can and should advance their distinctive visions of the common good within these private spheres, provided they do so in ways that also honor the same freedoms for all other persons, communities, and associations. Churches must not look to government, however, to advance their particular moral understandings unless they can demonstrate that the understandings in question are integral to the common social good.

Divisive conflicts provoked by the Christian Right, and more recently by Roman Catholic officials, have raised serious doubts about the abilities of faith-based communities and organizations to play constructive public roles in fostering a broader common good. Given these realities, the renewal of ecumenical Protestant social teaching requires attempts to build more constructive working relations with other Christian churches and religious bodies, demonstrating that religious diversity need not entail the fragmentation of civil society. Ecumenical Protestant churches once constituted the "mainline" in the religious involvements of American people, but they now represent only one discrete group of religious bodies alongside a wide array of diverse religious communities. A formerly "Christian country," Diana Eck observes, has now become "the world's most religiously diverse nation." It embraces multiple Christian traditions, diverse expressions of Jewish fidelity, a growing Muslim presence, and Buddhist and Hindu communities as well.[35] It should not be surprising that this diversity has stimulated interest in "new age" religious expressions as well, which encourage personal experimentations in the quest for spiritual wholeness. In his study, *Religion and Politics in the United States*, Kenneth Wald focuses attention on five discrete religious groups, all of which presently play a role in the public life of the nation: ecumenical Protestants, Roman Catholics, evangelical Protestants—most of whom consider themselves "conservatives," but some of whom are self-consciously "progressive"—African American churches, and the Jewish community, which embraces its own forms of diversity.[36]

In the late nineteenth and early twentieth centuries, ecumenical Protestants had a tendency to ignore other religious voices, presenting themselves as spokespersons for an enlightened religious establishment. They now have productive working relationships with independent African American churches, and they have welcomed Orthodox Churches into the National

35. Diana L. Eck, *A New Religious America: How a "Christian Country" Has Now Become the World's Most Religiously Diverse Nation* (New York: HarperSanFranciso, 2001). See also Eck's study, *On Common Ground: World Religions in America* (New York: Columbia University Press, 1997.)

36. Kenneth D. Wald, *Religion and Politics in the United States* (New York: St. Martin's, 1986), 182–265.

Council of Churches and the World Council of Churches.[37] They have pursued collaborative activities with Jewish communities on human rights issues, especially in response to the vicious cruelties of the Nazi Holocaust.[38] Following World War II, Ecumenical Protestant leaders warmly embraced the establishment of the state of Israel, and they continue to urge a viable two-state solution in Palestine, one that can end recurring cycles of violence between Israelis and Palestinians.

During the closing decades of the twentieth century ecumenical Protestants achieved new levels of agreement with Roman Catholic teachings on the major social issues of the day: nuclear disarmament, world peace, economic justice, and human rights. With regard to nuclear disarmament and world peace, there are striking similarities between the pastoral letter of the National Council of Catholic Bishops, *The Challenge of Peace: God's Promise and Our Response* (1983) and the pastoral letter of the United Methodist Bishops, *In Defense of Creation: The Nuclear Crisis and a Just Peace* (1986).[39] Similar parallels are manifest in public declarations on economic justice and human rights.[40] Just as the pro-life message of the Roman Catholic Church overlaps with the evangelical Protestant legacy of the Christian Right, so Roman Catholic teachings on economic policies and international relations are highly congruent with ecumenical Protestant social teachings. The ecumenical Protestant legacy of interdenominational and interfaith collaboration can itself be an important resource for addressing persistent public conflicts with the Christian Right and with the pro-life message of the Roman Catholic Church. These latter conflicts, I have argued, are not primarily about moral

37. See in particular Vigen Guroian, *Ethics after Christendom: Toward an Ecclesial Christian Ethics* (Grand Rapids: Eerdmans Publishing Co., 1994), and Alexander F. Webster, *The Price of Prophecy: Orthodox Churches on Peace, Freedom, and Security* (Grand Rapids: Eerdmans Publishing Co., 1995). With regard to distinctive African American traditions, see Peter J. Paris, *The Social Teaching of the Black Churches* (Philadelphia: Fortress Press, 1985).

38. See, for example, the papers of the 1979 Bernhard E. Olson Scholar's Conference on "The Church Struggle and the Holocaust" in Michael D. Ryan, ed., *Human Responses to the Holocaust: Perpetrators and Victims, Bystanders and Resisters* (New York: The Edwin Mellen Press, 1981). This conference was sponsored by The National Conference of Christians and Jews.

39. The Catholic Bishops' statement was published by the United States Catholic Conference (Washington, D.C.). The United Methodist Bishops' statement was published by The Graded Press (Nashville). Drawing upon evangelical Protestant resources, Ronald J. Sider and Richard K. Taylor had already ventured a similar statement, *Nuclear Holocaust and the Christian Hope: A Book for Christian Peacemakers* (New York: Paulist Press, 1982).

40. Especially important are Roman Catholic Papal Encyclicals on economic justice, for example, *Rerum Novarum: The Condition of Labor; Quadragesimo Anno: After Forty Years* (i.e., forty years after *Rerum Novarum*); *Laborem Exercens: On Human Work;* and *Centesimus Annus: On the Hundredth Anniversary of Rerum Novarum.* To these Encyclicals must be added the U.S. Catholic bishops' pastoral, *Economic Justice for All: Pastoral Letter on Catholic Social Teaching and the U.S. Economy* (Washington, D.C.: U.S. Catholic Conference, 1986). These resources are readily available in David J. O'Brien and

substance as such, but rather about the appropriate roles that Christian social teaching can and should play in a liberal democracy, one that rigorously limits legitimate government intrusion into private spheres of life.

With regard to the substantive content of Christian social teaching, the scope of relevant issues is vast, embracing economic policies, international relationships, efforts to advance human rights, military responses to terrorist threats and to ethnic and religious conflicts, projects of conflict resolution and peace making, and initiatives to protect the natural environment. For a comprehensive social vision, study documents associated with successive assemblies of the World Council of Churches have taken on special importance. The Sixth Assembly of the World Council of Churches, meeting in Vancouver, Canada (1983), formally adopted an ecumenical document on *Justice, Peace, and the Integrity of Creation.*[41] This document stressed moral guidelines for a "participatory society" that is "ecologically responsible" and "economically just." In 1990 "Justice, Peace, and the Integrity of Creation" (JPIC) furnished the organizing theme for a World Convocation meeting in Seoul, Korea. The Convocation incorporated into ecumenical Protestant teaching a motif from Latin American Liberation Theology, namely, the "preferential option for the poor," a theme also embraced by U.S. Catholic Bishops in their pastoral letter on the economy. The Convocation in Seoul specifically linked the "preferential option for the poor" to the liberation of developing nations from bondage to foreign debt. Building upon this witness, the Seventh Assembly that gathered in Canberra, Australia (1991), condemned "flagrant international inequality" and the "totally irresponsible exploitation of the created world." Increased attention to environmental concerns has been a noteworthy new development in Christian social teaching, one that only began to emerge in the seventies.[42] Within Protestantism, of course, resources produced by

---

Thomas A. Shannon, eds., *Catholic Social Thought: The Documentary Heritage* (Maryknoll, NY: Orbis, 1995). For an insightful overview, see David Hollenbach, *Justice, Peace, and Human Rights: American Catholic Social Ethics in a Pluralistic World* (New York: Crossroad, 1989). For an ecumenical Protestant counterpart, see Michael Kinnemon and Brian E. Cope, eds., *The Ecumenical Movement: An Anthology of Key Texts and Voices* (Grand Rapids: Eerdmans Publishing Company, 1997), and Dieter Hessel, ed., *The Church's Public Role* (Grand Rapids: Eerdmans Publishing Company, 1993). For a counter voice, see Stanley Hauerwas, *After Christendom? How the Church Is to Behave if Freedom, Justice, and a Christian Nation Are Bad Ideas* (Nashville: Abingdon Press, 1991).

41. The full title of the document is *Justice, Peace, and the Integrity of Creation: A Call to Common Commitments on Issues That Are Urgent for the Survival of Humankind* (Geneva: World Council of Churches, 1987). See also *Justice, Peace, and the Integrity of Creation: Insights from Orthodoxy*, ed. by Gennadios Limouris (Geneva: WCC Publications, 1990).

42. For a convenient summary of these developments, see the "Study Document" produced by the World Council of Churches "Advisory Group on Economic Matters" (AGEM), *Christian Faith and the*

ecumenical assemblies and convocations do not have recognized authority as official church teaching. They represent the fruits of vigorous conversations among delegates representing a range of ecumenical Protestant denominations, utilizing resources produced by advisory groups with expertise in the issues under study. To gain practical importance, documents of this kind have to be incorporated into the ongoing efforts of local congregations and denominational bodies to clarify their own sense of public responsibility within a complex world. Here too denominational and ecumenical agencies and special interest groups play indispensable roles in the implementation of an effective public witness.

In practical terms, comprehensive ventures in Christian social teaching must be narrowed to a set of more specific priorities, preferably to issues that have already gained public visibility in various kinds of political struggles. Issues of this kind are more likely to offer timely opportunities for making a difference in a sinful and flawed world. At the same time, situations of grave social injustice may call for some kind of prophetic testimony, even when there are no realistic prospects for overcoming the underlying problems. Amos, Hosea, and Micah, for example, attempted to expose social injustices perpetrated by Israelite monarchs and the class systems they embraced despite the fact that they were not in any position to propose practical solutions for overcoming those injustices. Disclosure is at least an indispensable first step in any social witness.

In the final analysis, a Christian social witness requires independent organizations that are focused upon a specific political agenda. This agenda requires them to distance themselves from the distinctively spiritual mission of congregations and denominational bodies. On this point, the Christian Right, in particular, The Christian Coalition, has furnished a realistic model of what is required. To be effective, moreover, activist organizations have to find ways of building coalitions with other political organizations, even when those organizations have priorities that are not fully in accord with Christian teachings. In a democratic society, coalition building is one dimension of Ernst Troeltsch's insistence upon the necessity of "compromise" in Christian social teaching. An appropriate compromise requires a constructive synthesis of cultural values that can fruitfully integrate distinctively Christian insights into a society's reigning civilizational ethic.[43]

World Economy Today (Geneva, Switzerland: WCC Publications, 1992). For an evangelical Protestant counterpart, see "The Oxford Declaration on Christian Faith and Economics" in Herbert Schlossberg, Vinay Samuel, and Ronald J. Sider, eds., *Christianity and Economics in the Post-Cold War Era: The Oxford Declaration and Beyond* (Grand Rapids: Eerdman's Publishing Company, 1994).

43. These matters are, of course, explicitly elaborated in chapter 2.

Ecumenical Protestant churches cannot make an effective social witness if they attempt to address every issue of public importance. They must discipline themselves to set clear priorities for their social message. They must study with diligence the issues they judge to be of paramount importance at a particular moment in time, critically weighing the moral and technical aspects of those issues so that their studies are not merely theoretical enterprises isolated from concrete political realities. As in the case of Dr. Martin Luther King Jr., there will be occasions when the struggle for justice will require "militant non-violent direct action" in order to open the way for substantive social changes. Commitments to building and maintaining strong congregational bases for a Christian public witness remain indispensable, so that the church's public witness remains a credible expression of its worldly mission. Efforts in these directions will not lead to a Christian America, still less to a Christian world, but they can contribute to the amelioration of human suffering, and in so doing witness to the Christ who meets us in the destitution suffered by the "least" of our brothers and sisters. These efforts will also help us understand more fully the meaning of being the Church of Jesus Christ amid the troubles of a fallen world.

Chapter 6

Faith, Culture, and Power

Reflections on James H. Cone's *Martin & Malcolm & America: A Dream or a Nightmare*

*J*ames H. Cone's contributions to theological education and to the public vocation of the churches have been immense: from the bold advocacy of black power in his first book,[1] through his careful retrieval of the texts and traditions of black liberation thought,[2] to his disciplined efforts to deepen the dialogue among various liberation traditions within a global context.[3] He continually travels untrod paths. He does not shrink back from making himself vulnerable to criticism from those who speak out of different cultures and experiences. He strives always to remain connected with the practical struggles of people, especially those who have been victims of oppression. Happily, his writings are invariably clear, rhetorically powerful, and full of passion.

Of all of Cone's books, however, *Martin & Malcolm & America* may prove to have the most enduring value. This book is important not simply because of the intrinsic merit of its subject matter, nor because of its skillful handling of the ideas, experiences, and activities of these two extraordinary leaders. It is important because of the way it portrays theological inquiry.

In his treatments of the Rev. Dr. Martin Luther King Jr. and the Rev. Malcolm X, Cone highlights forms of theology that are: a) practice-based yet deeply rooted in living traditions of faith and practice: b) attentive to the conditioning and shaping power of social and cultural dynamics, but without reducing thought to a mere function of these dynamics: c) attuned to the importance of organizational and institutional structures, both as barriers to

---

1. James Cone, *Black Theology & Black Power* (New York: The Seabury Press, 1969).
2. James Cone, *Speaking the Truth: Ecumenism, Liberation, and Black Theology* (Grand Rapids, MI: William B. Eerdmans, 1986) and Gayraud Wilmore and James Cone, *Black Theology: A Documentary History, 1966–79.* (Maryknoll, NY: Orbis Books, 1979).
3. James Cone, *My Soul Looks Back* (Nashville: Abingdon Press, 1982), 93–113. *Black Theology: A Documentary History*, 445–601.

and as resources for liberating actions, and d) substantively joined to the promotion of human dignity and social justice.

Not surprisingly, the theological issues which come into focus as a result of Cone's investigations are profound and fundamental, not merely academically interesting or fashionable. I want to focus on two: 1) the relation of a redemptive and liberating religious message—whether Christian or Muslim—to the cultural materials that shape concrete human appropriations of that message, and 2) the relation of elemental religious convictions to sociopolitical commitments to human dignity, justice, and freedom.

The Cultural Penetration of Distinctively Religious Understandings

I want to begin by citing my colleague, Lamin Sanneh, a native Gambian who grew up in an influential Muslim family yet converted as a young adult to evangelical Protestantism. In a recent monograph, Sanneh argues for the essential translatability of the Christian message.[4] By its very nature, he contends, the Gospel finds expression in a multiplicity of languages and cultures. No single expression is privileged, still less final. Many, if not all, have the potential of becoming authentic vehicles of the saving, liberating Gospel. Paul's dictum, *neither* Jew nor Greek, is at the same time a positive declaration: both Jew and Greek, and so likewise, Macedonian, European, African, Asian, and Pacific Islander.

Any particular appropriation of the Christian message, Sanneh argues further, involves the assimilation into Christian understandings of cultural materials that shape a given social context. His point is that indigenization is not simply a late twentieth-century invention. It is a fundamental feature of the Christian world mission. This fact is often obscured in treatments of European Christianity since the adaptations of Christianity to Hellenistic, Latin, and European cultures was largely complete more than a millennium ago. Yet Christianity does not exist except in culturally indigenized forms.

The difficulty is this: any indigenous appropriation of the Christian message will inevitably reflect the limitations, ambiguities, and deceits that mark the culture in question. To be sure, the Christian message promises to transform and renew every culture it touches. It evokes in diverse human cultures unrealized possibilities for development. Those possibilities in turn give human beings a new vantage point on the Gospel itself. Indigenization,

---

4. Lamin Sanneh, *Translating the Message: The Missionary Impact on Culture* (Maryknoll, NY: Orbis Books, 1989).

then, both facilitates the hearing of the Gospel and qualifies the manner of that hearing. No particular reception of the Gospel can ever claim more than relative and partial truth, and every reception stands in need of correction and supplementation by alternative perspectives. Further, every hearing is ambiguous, flawed, even distorted, and hence, in need of prophetic criticism and transformation, both from within and from the perspective of alternative views.

The activities and reflections of King and Malcolm X compel theological attention to these complex and difficult matters. King, for example, was nurtured in one of the central streams of an independent African-American Christianity. This stream of tradition disposed him to take for granted a non-racist appropriation of the Christian message. Peter Paris refers to this non-racist reading as the "Black Christian principle," a belief in the kinship of all peoples as brothers and sisters in relation to the parenthood of God.[5] Correctly presuming the universal import of the Christian message, King sought to relate his own spiritual heritage to the intellectual accomplishments of white, liberal Protestant Christianity. Even though he knew the pervasiveness of racism in American culture, he expected that white Protestantism would at least be receptive to a moral challenge to renounce its acquiescence in the racism of the larger society.

It was only with reluctance that King faced the degree to which Euro-American ethnocentrism disposed white Christians in America not only to accept, but even to advocate racist appropriations of the Gospel. To this day, most theology done by white Americans continues to treat African-American Christian traditions as little more than relatively naive and unsophisticated variants of white evangelical Protestantism. There is a general failure to appreciate the distinctive power and originality of these traditions and their indispensable contributions to the integrity of the Christian mission.

In confronting the depth of the racist assumptions in white American Christianity, King gained a heightened awareness of the positive contributions to African-American Christian consciousness of traditional African religion and of the tenacious struggles of African peoples to survive the evils of slavery. Central to African-American Christianity is its clear grasp of the race-transcending universalism of the Christian Gospel. Thus, King discovered that what he had initially taken for granted was actually an extraordinary religio-cultural accomplishment.

More bluntly than King, Malcolm X exposed the inherent racism of white Christianity in America. He could only conclude that Christianity is a "white-

---

5. Paris, Peter J., *The Social Teachings of the Black Church* (Philadelphia: Fortress Press, 1985).

man's" religion, whose function for Black Americans was to domesticate them and turn them into pet animals. To claim their full humanity and dignity, Malcolm X argued, Black people require a Black religion, one with African roots. In drawing this conclusion, he too may have failed to discern the distinctiveness of African-American Christianity.

Without diminishing the compelling logic of Malcolm X's exposure of white, American Christianity, Cone also notes that the Nation of Islam did not arise from contact between Black Americans and Muslims. Its proximate origins were nationalist movements within African-American Christianity, especially that of Marcus Garvey. African-American Christianity had already dealt with the problem of Malcolm X's radical critique of American Christianity. Yet it had addressed that problem largely by means of African-American Christian resources, in particular, resources that thematized the African social and cultural contribution to the distinctive African-American appropriation of the Gospel.

Peter Paris has shown that, from time to time, the leaders of the independent African-American churches expressly stated that the empowerment and liberation of Black Americans was of more fundamental importance than explicit Christian identification as such.[6] If Christian America would not renounce its racism, then perhaps African Americans would find a non-racist religious alternative.

In the course of his public ministry, Malcolm X became increasingly aware of the fact that the Nation of Islam is not the same as orthodox Islam. In the spirit of inherent translatability, he claimed that the Nation of Islam was a distinctive appropriation of Islam suited to the social and cultural circumstances of Black Americans. At the same time, his desire to make contact with historic Islam also grew. Among other things, he arranged for Elijah Muhammad to go on holy pilgrimage to Mecca as a recognized Islamic leader. The final stage of Malcolm X's own odyssey occurred when he broke with the Nation of Islam, affiliated with an orthodox mosque, and adopted orthodox Islamic observances.

Ironically, Malcolm X's move to orthodox Islam might eventually have had the effect of distancing him from the distinctive travail of Black Americans and their religious practices. Lamin Sanneh, who is also a specialist in Islamic studies, observes that Islam, unlike Christianity, is not readily translatable into a multiplicity of cultures. To become Muslim is to become Arabic: it is to learn Arabic in order to study the Quran in its true, revealed language: and it is to adopt Arabic customs and practices in one's everyday

6. Paris, 50–52.

life. Sanneh's observation should not be taken too literally. There are manifestly divergent Islamic parties, and Islam, like any world religion, adapts to some degree to various local and regional cultures as it spreads to different parts of the world. Sanneh's point is that such cultural adaptation is intrinsically appropriate in the case of Christianity, but religiously more problematic in the case of Islam. The diverse tendencies in these religions qualify their respective patterns of acculturation.

Islam's Arabic cultural base appears not to have inhibited its spread, either in Africa or in urban centers within the United States. In Africa, at least, Islam does seem to have complicated the efforts of relatively young, multi-cultural African states to develop a distinctive and cohesive national identity, one capable of sustaining social and political development over time. Based on Sanneh's analysis, one can anticipate that the Arabic nature of Islam would in time also complicate the efforts of African Americans to claim an authentic American identity. In this respect, the Nation of Islam, despite its curious historical inventions, may have been more functional for African Americans than historic Islam. Though Islam may offer African Americans freedom from the deep racist assumptions that pervade American Christianity, it could in the long run lead to its own forms of cultural alienation.

Cone's study dramatizes the practical import of the faith-culture question for theological inquiry. It renders urgent the need for attending systematically to these dynamics in the interest of bringing to the fore the liberating, world-transforming promise of the Christian message.

Faith and Justice

The second major set of issues concerns the relation between basic religious convictions and public responsibility for social justice and human well-being. These issues are especially difficult where the public life of a society is formally secular and religiously pluralistic. In such a society, there can be no direct transfer of discrete religious convictions to public policies and practices.

Cone observes that Malcolm X's religion *was* his preoccupation with justice. For King, he suggests, the quest for justice was an essential implication of faith. More important, it would seem, is that justice for Malcolm X and King moved in two different directions, at least in the early phases of their public activities. For King, the focal interest was public policy, initially the right of all Americans to the ballot and to full access to public accommodations. These goals were largely achieved through federal civil rights legislation in 1965 and 1966.

In the last years of his life King gave increasing attention to economic issues, especially the right to a job with decent pay and good benefits, and the right to a quality education. Concern for housing, health care, and other social goods was also in the picture. King's assassination, Cone reminds us, occurred in the context of his support for sanitation workers in their dispute with the city of Memphis.

In turning to problems of poverty, King became increasingly aware of class factors in the sufferings of African Americans. He expressed sympathy for socialist ideas, though, as Cone notes, he did not undertake any systematic studies in class analysis. Besides, his interest in poverty was by no means single-minded. He devoted considerable energy toward ending the war in Vietnam.

As a minister of the Nation of Islam, Malcolm X emphasized Black consciousness, Black pride, Black discipline, and Black economic and social self-development. Acutely aware of the harsh realities of class, his response was to stress discipline and self-development. He also promoted Black resistance to the unjust and insulting treatment of Black Americans, even sanctioning the use of violence in self-defense. Yet his own practice remained as consistently non-violent as King's!

During the early years of his public activity, Malcolm X did not concern himself with public policy. In racist America, he believed, such an interest would be naive, fruitless, even self-demeaning. He ridiculed King for his vision of justice and for his programmatic activities. His tendencies toward political activism were curbed, moreover, by Elijah Muhammad. The more Malcolm X gained public notoriety, the more aggressively Elijah Muhammad sought to restrain his political activities.

After breaking with the Nation of Islam, Malcolm X moved closer to King's political involvements. Alongside an ongoing commitment to Black autonomy and self-development, he took greater interest in the promotion of civil liberties within the larger American society. In so doing, he displayed more tolerance for the ambiguities of American politics.

In this new context, Malcolm X had to surrender any simple identification of justice with religious commitment. Though he continued to present himself as a Muslim minister, he found it necessary to create explicitly political organizations that could unite people with a diversity of religious and secular sensibilities. What bound people together in these new organizations was not religion, but a common determination to promote justice and freedom for Black Americans.

For religious leaders who would seek to play an effective public role the central critical questions are two. First, how do religious communities—

whether Christian, Muslim, or Jewish—properly play a role in fostering justice and human well-being within a secular religiously plural society? Second, what forms of public law and public policy can actually bring about justice and human well-being in post-industrial, post-modern societies?

When religious people enter the public arena, must they bracket their distinctive faith identities in order to uncover common ground among like-minded people across a diversity of religious and secular views? If common ground can be found, moreover, will it furnish normative conceptions of justice and human well-being capable of guiding public actions? Might this common ground be provided by the American civil religion, as some have argued? Can the American civil religion sustain a viable public ethic alongside of discrete conceptions of religious ethics? If the American civil religion, however, is too tainted with racism to serve as a vehicle for relative justice in human society, is there a public ethic that is common to African-American communities and to other racial, ethnic, and religious minorities—perhaps a special way of understanding the American civil religion itself? Alternatively, are there some authentic and practical ways in which discrete religious traditions within a religiously plural society might substantively figure in a public discourse about the common good? When we confront questions such as these, we soon discover that it is far easier to talk about the essential unity of faith and justice than to find practical, faith-informed ways of promoting justice in a secular, religiously plural society.[7]

The second set of issues has to do with the formulation of public policies that can actually promote human justice and well-being in a post-industrial, post-modern society. What can we do to mitigate persisting problems of poverty, human degradation, and racism in contemporary American society? What courses of action will make a difference?

Poverty and human degradation hardly confront us with simple problems that we can readily solve if we only have the requisite determination! Indeed, there would appear to be no single analysis of the causes of such suffering that can grasp all of the relevant factors, still less trace their multiple interrelationships. Similarly, there is no readily identifiable set of policy initiatives that can effectively reverse processes that lead to such suffering. Furthermore, even if we could discover promising directions to take, we would still face the task of building a public consensus in support of those initiatives. These dif-

---

7. Cf. Thomas W. Ogletree, "Renewing Ecumenical Protestant Social Teaching," in Peter Paris and Douglas Knight, eds. *Justice and the Holy* (Atlanta: Scholars Press, 1989), 338–405 [reprinted as chapter 5 in this volume], and "The Public Witness of the Christian Churches: Reflections Based upon Ernst Troeltsch's *Social Teachings of the Christian Church*," *The Annual Society of Christian Ethics*, 43–74 [reprinted as chapter 2 in this volume].

ficulties are not cited to dramatize the hopelessness of the present situation. They are lifted up in order to make clear the critical studies required for the practical implementation of key features in the legacies of Martin Luther King Jr. and Malcolm X.

Cone's study of King and Malcolm X heightens our appreciation for these two singular leaders. Cone will not have achieved his purposes, however, if he merely prompts us to add their names to our list of saints and heroes. His study presses us toward new forms of critical inquiry and practical experimentation in support of an ongoing struggle for justice, dignity, and human well-being in a world set free from the evils and cruelties of racism.

Appendix

The Ecclesial Context of Christian Ethics

Presidential Address to the Society of Christian Ethics (1984)

*T*his meeting marks the twenty-fifth anniversary of our Society. It is remarkable that an association so young has already become so vital and so integral to work in our field. To speak personally, when a small group of professors of Christian social ethics first organized themselves as a scholarly guild, I was in my final year of seminary and preparing for graduate study. The Society is scarcely older than my career as a scholar and a teacher; yet when I first came in contact with it, I experienced it as a necessary feature in the professional life of any serious student of Christian ethics.

The Society has changed dramatically in these twenty-five years. From its origins in "mainline" Protestant traditions, it has become an ecumenical association. It now has representatives from most of the branches of North American Christianity, and it reaches out tentatively to the thoughtful study of other religions as well, especially Judaism and Islam. Beginning as an association for seminary professors, its center of gravity has shifted to embrace the interests of departments of religious studies in state universities and liberal arts colleges. In addition, the Society counts among its members a small number of professionals from outside of the academy, especially in church agencies, but also in law, business, government, health care, and in grass-roots organizing activity among oppressed peoples. Initially functioning, though without conscious intent, as a privileged domain for white male scholars, it has moved persistently toward the concrete embodiment of its commitment to racial and sexual inclusiveness, and of increasing global awareness as well.[1]

These shifts have not taken place without stress to our corporate identity, especially when some among us have suggested that the term Christian is too

---

1. These shifts in orientation and in membership composition are outlined in the forthcoming history of the Society of Christian Ethics by Edward L. Long Jr., tentatively entitled, *Academic Bonding and Social Concerns: The Society of Christian Ethics, 1959–1983*. The volume will be published as one of the studies in religious ethics of the *Journal of Religious Ethics*.

restrictive to encompass our interests and activities. Given our diversity, most of us would be hard-pressed to specify what it is that holds us together. Yet a spirit of collegiality, intellectual vitality, and moral passion marks our life as an association. Our differences repeatedly prove to be invigorating rather than divisive.

What is especially remarkable is that we enjoy vitality as an association even though our grasp of the subject matter which formally brings us together is uncertain. Indeed, it may not be too much to say that we are perilously close to losing our subject matter, that is, Christian ethics as a distinctive, normative inquiry capable of making a substantive contribution to the contemporary human quest for moral wisdom and understanding.

I want to dramatize our collective difficulties in dealing constructively with Christian ethics as a critical perspective on the moral life. My observations are by no means intended to suggest that there are none among us who are doing original and creative thinking in Christian ethics. I mean rather to speak to our difficulties as a guild in identifying a social location capable of bestowing significance upon our activities as students and teachers of Christian ethics.

I shall be arguing that Christian thinking about the moral life requires for its integrity and power an ecclesial context. Such thinking, that is to say, emerges out of personal participation in a community of faith enduring over time. This community is marked by shared understandings of the ultimate nature of things and the meaning of the human pilgrimage in relation to what is finally real. It articulates these understandings in story and myth, and reiterates them in appropriate ritual activity. It summons participants to embody them in their personal lives, and to enact them in concrete practice in a social world. It nurtures the young, and any new members, in these common understandings and the forms of life to which they are related. Christian ethical thinking cut off from a lively involvement with ecclesial existence is abstract and impotent. It is nothing more than a collection of intellectual constructions by creative individuals, having only accidental connection with the experiences and perceptions of others.[2]

My suggestion is that we have difficulty with the normative development of Christian ethics because we have difficulty dealing with the ecclesial reality which is necessary to that development. Ironically, this latter difficulty may be

---

2. The notion of an ecclesial context is taken from the foundational work of Edward Farley. See especially his *Ecclesial Man: A Social Phenomenology of Faith and Reality* (Philadelphia: Fortress Press, 1975), and also the more recent *Ecclesial Reflections: An Anatomy of Theological Method* (Philadelphia: Fortress Press, 1982).

directly related to our energy as an association. Ethics claims the attention of many members of our association because of a moral passion to deal with the major social problems of our present-day world. We recognize that the issues most decisively affecting the lives of people in our time transcend the concrete reality of the church as we know it. We hunger to address the larger issues, to contribute to the struggle for social justice in a wider social context. The moral wisdom we seek is that capable of guiding us in this struggle.

This orientation is continuous with our history as an association. We were, after all, founded as a society of Christian *social* ethics. Our founders represented either an ongoing commitment to the social gospel, perhaps under the aegis of the concept "responsible society," or they identified with Reinhold Niebuhr's advocacy of Christian realism. In both cases the preoccupation was with the witness of Christian faith to issues in the larger society. The ecclesial context of Christian ethics was not so much ignored as taken for granted. As a theme for inquiry, it was largely subordinate to social questions.

For the most part, we have not been content to define our task as the moral guidance of Christian communities and congregations. As a result of powerful social forces, such communities have come to have significance chiefly in the private sector, in relation to families and residential neighborhoods. Given this confinement, they have had little direct access to the great social questions of the day. In many instances they have become places of escape from disturbing realities in modern society, encouraging nostalgic attachments to former ways of life, nurturing destructive prejudices, reinforcing provincial viewpoints, furnishing moral and religious justifications for advantaged classes, and abandoning the victims of social dislocation in rapidly changing urban environments. To put the point baldly, most of the Christian congregations we know firsthand are not disposed to share the passion for social justice which many of us profess. They appear more interested in maintaining secure spaces which can sustain them in their attempts to cope with the daily problems of living. While most of us can readily acknowledge our own stake in this interest, it falls short of our self-conscious commitments.

As congregations have become more distant from the major social questions of the day, so have the traditions of moral understanding which they mediate. Indeed, popular interpretations of these traditions associate them almost exclusively with personal morality, especially as it is lived out in the private sector. Insofar as we strive to address the central problems of post-industrial society, we necessarily commit ourselves to learning a language and a way of thinking which are appropriate to the basic institutions of that society. Distinctively Christian thinking is not manifestly relevant to that enterprise. Alasdair MacIntyre has defined our dilemma sharply. "Either [moral theology] will remain within the theological closed circle: in which case it will have no access to the public and shared moral criteria of our society. Or it will accept those criteria: in which case it may well have important things to say, but these will not be distinctively Christian."[3]

Earlier work in Christian social ethics did not confront this dilemma so directly since the common culture continued to give a certain prominence to Christian orientations. Yet Christian social ethics may also have obscured the dilemma by functioning at a high level of generality. It analyzed the elements of justice in the traditions forming the greater American community and then related these elements to Christian notions of love, not a particularly difficult undertaking. At this level it was apparently able to accomplish a Christian transformation of cultural materials.

However, if we are to address the crucial issues which currently trouble our social existence, we can no longer content ourselves with merely reiterating and reinterpreting the grand themes of our predecessors. We have to pursue our reflections in a manner that is much closer to the organizational contexts within which human beings actually function, and that also means in forms of discourse which have manifest pertinence to those contexts. To be more specific: political ethics must give way to policy ethics, and policy ethics must find a place for itself within policy studies generally. To become involved in policy studies, moreover, is to become a specialist in a given region of policy making: energy, urban affairs, disarmament, primary and secondary education. Economic ethics likewise becomes an aspect of policy ethics, or else it seeks entry to business and industrial corporations as management ethics.

---

3. Alasdair MacIntyre, *Against the Self Images of the Age* (Notre Dame, IN: University of Notre Dame Press, 1978), p. 23.

This formulation of the problem counts more heavily against Protestant than Roman Catholic ethics. Catholic thought has a well-established tradition of distinguishing between natural and supernatural understandings in ethics. This distinction permits it to participate fully in a public discourse while maintaining the authority of the over-arching framework of thought provided by the church's teaching. Roman Catholic ethics has, however, been troubled by the ambiguous status of the natural. Is the content of natural morality wholly determined through a public moral discourse which is governed by rational analysis and argument? Or does it at critical points require the support of the *Magisterium*? If the latter, on what grounds can the authoritative teaching of the church resolve disputes over natural law? Finally, in Roman Catholic thought the ecclesial context of a distinctively Christian ethic resides more in the Church's teaching office, broadly or narrowly conceived, than in the concrete matrix of communal interactions. The more this teaching authority is dispersed throughout the concrete life of the Church, the more the situation of Roman Catholic ethics approximates that of contemporary Protestant ethics.

For a discussion of these issues see the collection edited by Charles E. Curran and Richard A. McCormick entitled *Readings in Moral Theology No. 2: The Distinctiveness of Christian Ethics* (New York: Paulist Press, 1980). See also Charles E. Curran, *Themes in Fundamental Moral Theology* (Notre Dame, IN: University of Notre Dame Press, 1977), especially the chapters on "Natural Law," "Church Law," and "Ethical Methodology and Church Teaching."

Medical ethics directs us to the clinical practice of health care professionals, or perhaps to the teaching and research activities of medical schools. Analogous points could be made about legal ethics or the ethics of criminal justice or any other specialized interest we may elect to pursue.

The principal point is that the more organizational and institutional settings of a public sort provide the social location within which our relevant research and thinking occur, the more our reflections lose their distinctively Christian character. We become highly specialized students of particular facets of modern life. Our work takes on characteristics of the human sciences, though harnessed to policy questions and qualified by attention to philosophical analyses of ethical issues raised by those policy questions. Centers for policy studies, whether university-related, government-related, or free-standing, provide the controlling paradigms for the social organization of ethical inquiry.

This picture is not likely to be substantially altered even if we pursue our professional interests as participants in the instructional programs of universities and seminaries, or perhaps as staff members of denominational boards of church and society. Even in these settings our approach to Christian ethics is apt to be governed by the conceptions we have of the way ethical analysis becomes germane to the problems of the social world. To be sure, denominational pronouncements on public issues invariably contain broad theological warrants for the positions they take, and they normally utilize some of the general categories which have traditionally belonged to Christian social ethics. However, insofar as they are addressed to policy makers, perhaps as position papers for church lobbyists in Washington, they too must approximate the sophistication and the specialized knowledge characteristic of current policy studies. Moreover, the normative understandings they embody must find expression in a discourse which is actually or potentially operative in the relevant organizational settings. Under these circumstances it is hardly surprising that Christian ethics comes to be identified with personal ethics, and that social ethics virtually ceases to be Christian at all.

Within the Society of Christian Ethics, our recent attempts to participate in a normative public discourse have usually taken one of two directions. On the one hand, we have made appeals to moral understandings ingredient in the greater American community, e.g., the Constitution of the United States, or the American "civil religion." On the other hand, we have utilized constructive philosophical formulations, represented by thinkers such as William Frankena, R. M. Hare, Stephen Toulmin, or more recently, John Rawls, Alan Gewirth, and Alan Donegan. These thinkers utilize modes of reasoning which in principle are open to all human beings, or at least to all human beings nurtured in what we broadly identify as western culture. Our Christian thinking, where it appears at all, has tended to consist of theological appeals which authorize the use of non-Christian materials. These appeals furnish adherents of Christian faith with ultimate warrants for honoring the moral norms under consideration, and with subjective motivation for embodying them in concrete living.

We can sharpen the dilemma further still. Even when specifically Christian norms, such as neighbor love, are scrutinized with the aid of philosophical analysis and argument, they too tend to lose their distinctiveness. In the process of analysis they are translated, virtually without remainder, into philosophical notions, for example, a concept of justice. One recalls in this connection Gene Outka's characterization of *agape* as "equal regard."[4] If Christian love differs from a general human obligation to do justice, it is only in its summons to works of supererogation, for example, a readiness to love the enemy, to go the second mile, to lay down one's life for a friend, to suffer injury at the hands of others without recompense.[5] Yet such works of supererogation are scarcely intelligible within the universe of discourse which has governed the analysis in the first place.

It is altogether appropriate that one of our distinguished colleagues, James Gustafson, should finally ask: Can ethics be Christian?[6] The question discloses the fact that the philosophical presuppositions which govern the public moral discourse of contemporary society do not readily allow for characteristic Christian insights. Despite its earlier hegemony in Western culture, Christian faith has once again become a minority stance in society, not unlike its position in the first and second centuries of our common era. Of course, Gustafson arrived at a positive answer to his question, but his question remains real and altogether serious.

We have not by any means all been ready to devote ourselves to some aspect of policy ethics or professional ethics. Despite its merits, many in our number have found this undertaking too restrictive. It entails working within the constraints imposed by the basic institutions of modern society. It does not permit us to raise questions about the constitutive principles of the institutions themselves. We have, therefore, sought ways to subject these institutions and their dominant value orientations to criticism. Gustafson describes this latter effort as the critique of ethos.[7] The critique of ethos takes a number of forms: the critique of the bureaucratization of life in high-technology civilization; the

4. Gene Outka, *Agape: An Ethical Analysis* (New Haven: Yale University Press, 1972), pp. 9–24, 260–74.

5. Ibid., pp. 294–97.

6. James M. Gustafson, *Can Ethics Be Christian?* (Chicago: University of Chicago Press, 1975).

7. James M. Gustafson, *Ethics from a Theocentric Perspective: Theology and Ethics* (Chicago: University of Chicago Press, 1981), p. 71.

critique of the modern confidence in science and technology for the solution of social problems; the critique of advanced capitalism, especially its imperialist forms; the critique of racist and sexist distortions of basic social institutions.[8] Gustafson's recent advocacy of a theocentric perspective in ethics itself constitutes a critique of ethos, though at an explicitly theological level.

The critique of ethos offers an attractive option for students of Christian ethics since it appears to take us to a more fundamental level of inquiry, one well suited to a religious orientation. Yet this option also has its problems. For one thing, its driving impulses are not necessarily linked any more directly to Christian understandings than are the moral reasonings of policy ethics. In its own way it, too, may amount to a surrendering of Christian perspectives in favor of modes of analysis more at home in the dominant culture. Moreover, its tendency, at least in the short run, is to render our reflections largely irrelevant to the way decisions are actually made and policies set in complex social organizations. Precisely because of its radicalism, ethos criticism is of little immediate help in concrete attempts to clarify and resolve social problems. Indeed, insofar as it is effective, its function may be to weaken our basic institutions and their organizational expressions, reducing their ability to carry out their social purposes. Predictably, the critique of ethos has now evoked neo-conservative apologies for ethos, contentions that existing social arrangements, despite their limitations, constitute the best forms of order we are likely to achieve in this morally ambiguous world.[9]

Gustafson calls attention to a deeper problem. He notes that ethos criticism requires a process of conversion, a transformation of perspective, which practically speaking is hard to achieve.[10] Ethos critics are social reformers. However, if we take account of the socialization processes of culture and society, we cannot readily apprehend the points of explicit activity to which we might turn our reforming zeal. How, Gustafson is asking, are we to enact ethos criticism in practice? If the casuists—the category includes students of policy

8. There are many excellent examples of such literature, including: John C. Bennett, *The Radical Imperative: From Theology to Social Ethics* (Philadelphia: Westminster Press, 1975); Daniel C. Maguire, *A New American Justice: Ending the White Male Monopolies* (Garden City, NY: Doubleday, 1980); and Gibson Winter, *Liberating Creation: Foundations of Religious Social Ethics* (New York: Crossroad, 1981). Works in liberation theology belong under this rubric, e.g., James H. Cone, *God of the Oppressed* (New York: Seabury Press, 1975); Rosemary Radford Ruether, *Sexism and God-Talk: Toward a Feminist Theology* (Boston: Beacon Press, 1983); and Cornel West, *Prophesy Deliverance! An Afro-American Revolutionary Christianity* (Philadelphia: Westminster Press, 1982). As an example of a study which combines policy ethics and ethos criticism in an illuminating way, see Roger Lincoln Shinn, *Forced Options: Social Decisions for the 21st Century* (San Francisco: Harper and Row, Publishers, 1982).

9. Cf. e.g., Michael Novak, *The American Vision: An Essay on the Future of Democratic Capitalism* (Washington, D.C., American Enterprise Institute for Public Policy Research, 1978).

10. Gustafson, *Ethics from a Theocentric Perspective*, p. 72.

ethics and professional ethics—"accept uncritically too many conditions of modern culture and society," he observes, "they at least have more precisely defined and definable issues to address."[11] He concludes by suggesting that the casuists and the critics of ethos need each other: "by pushing the casuists to theological margins one comes to questions of ethos; by pushing the ethos to its practical consequences one comes to casuistry."[12] Gustafson may have arrived at this friendly little dialectic a bit too easily, for the gap between the stances he identifies remains wide.

Nevertheless, Gustafson's observations about ethos criticism are essentially correct insofar as such criticism is abstracted from an ecclesial context. That is to say, ethos criticism is vague and largely without practical import if it does not emerge out of a communal context capable of sustaining an alternative way of perceiving and valuing the world and an alternative way of constituting social reality. The practice out of which ethos criticism arises, and to which it initially leads, is the formation and building up of communities that have different understandings of the world from those dominant in the basic institutions of modern society.

The point is self-evident to liberation thought. Radical criticism presupposes radical communities. Thus, Latin American liberation theologians speak of "base communities" as the social context for a re-visioning of the Christian message.[13] Feminist theologians in North America use the same notion to characterize the support communities required to sustain the critique of sexism in culture and society and to nurture the quest for egalitarian and non-hierarchical social alternatives.[14] Likewise, Black liberation thought could hardly exist without the long-term sustenance in the Black church of non-racist understandings of Christian faith and life. Though the dominant traditions of the Black church have not been nearly so radical as contemporary liberation theology, they have furnished the seed-bed within which such thought could grow and flourish.[15]

This analysis brings us to my central thesis: that constructive thinking in Christian ethics requires an ecclesial context. I can now add as well that such

11. Ibid.

12. Ibid.

13. See Ruether, *Sexism and God-Talk*, pp. 204–05. Quite appropriately, Juan Luis Segundo began his "theology for artisans of a new humanity" with the study, *The Community Called Church* (Maryknoll, NY: Orbis Books, 1973).

14. Ruether, *Sexism and God-Talk*, pp. 205–06.

15. Cf. e.g., Gayraud S. Wilmore, *Black Religion and Black Radicalism: An Interpretation of the Religious History of Afro-American People*, second ed., revised and enlarged (Maryknoll, NY: Orbis Books, 1973), and Peter Paris' *The Social Teaching of the Black Churches* (Philadelphia: Fortress Press, 1984).

a context can no longer be taken for granted. If we are to be interpreters of Christian ethics in our time, we will have to give fresh attention to the church as a community capable of sustaining a distinctive moral vision of the world. We shall also have to reexamine the social and institutional conditions which are requisite to its ongoing life in high-technology civilization. The intent of these inquiries is not to prepare the way for a withdrawal from the larger social world into a self-contained and autonomous socio-cultural system. Such a withdrawal would be incompatible with the universal outreach of Christian faith. It is rather to rediscover the wellspring of Christian thought, and to equip ourselves to draw upon the Christian legacy in addressing the moral problems of the age. Stated differently, the point is not to abandon social ethics, but to reclaim the possibility of a Christian contribution to social ethics.[16]

Ernst Troeltsch provides a fruitful guide for this undertaking.[17] To speak to the modern world, Troeltsch contends, Christian faith must find a way to combine its own distinctive ethos with an "ethic of civilization" suited to the dominant social forces at work in that world. Three elements are lifted up in this formulation: the dominant social forces of the modern world, the ethic of civilization which interacts with them, and the Christian ethos.[18] Troeltsch's Weberian social theory encompasses the first two elements. It keeps before us, on the one hand, the distinction between social forces and civilizational values, and, on the other, the essential interconnection of the two. The Christian ethos designates a normative possibility whose import for modern soci-

16. The ecclesial context of Christian ethics has not been wholly neglected in the last two decades. It would be appropriate to recall two volumes by Gibson Winter, *The Suburban Captivity of the Churches* (New York: The MacMillan Company, 1962) and *The New Creation as Metropolis* (New York: The MacMillan Company, 1963), and James M. Gustafson's *Treasure in Earthen Vessels* (New York: Harper & Row, Publishers, 1961). Pertinent also is Gustafson's collection of essays, *The Church as Moral Decision-Maker* (Philadelphia: The Pilgrim Press, 1970). Paul Lehmann's *Ethics in a Christian Context* (New York: Harper & Row, Publishers, 1963) begins with an account of the church as the "context of ethical reflection." See pp. 45–73. He does not, however, maintain the primacy of this orientation, moving instead to a political theology, and from there to an individual actor making concrete moral decisions in complex situations. Mention should be made of an elegant little book by James B. Nelson, *Moral Nexus: Ethics of Christian Identity and Community* (Philadelphia: The Westminster Press, 1971). Nelson has a solid theoretical grasp of the ecclesial context of ethics. His study has, unfortunately, gone out of print all too quickly. John Howard Yoder's *Politics of Jesus* (Grand Rapids, MI: William B. Eerdmans Publishing Company, 1972) is marked throughout by an ecclesial orientation. More recently Stanley Hauerwas has begun to attend systematically to the ecclesial context of Christian ethics, e.g., in the essays "The Church and Liberal Democracy: The Moral Limits of a Secular Polity" and "The Virtues and our Communities: Human Nature as History," both published in the collection, *A Community of Character: Toward a Constructive Christian Social Ethic* (Notre Dame, IN: University of Notre Dame Press, 1981), pp. 72–86, 111–28.

17. See especially Ernst Troeltsch, *The Social Teaching of the Christian Churches,* two vols., tr. Olive Wyon (New York: Harper Torchbooks, 1960).

18. Ibid., vol. 2, pp. 993–1013.

ety Troeltsch was seeking to assess. What is not here stated explicitly is that the Christian ethos itself requires for its existence viable forms of social organization. Troeltsch's church-sect typology is nothing other than his attempt to identify the primary modes of social organization which have been generated by Christian understandings. His work assumes throughout the necessity for Christian thought of an ecclesial context. With regard to social ethics, his leading theoretical insight is that Christian convictions gain significance for the life of a society not by impinging directly on the dominant economic and social forces at play in it, but by shaping, modifying, even transforming, its civilizational ethic.

Troeltsch was not particularly hopeful that Christian social thought could again take on "comprehensive historical significance," certainly not in the sense of medieval Catholicism or seventeenth-century Calvinism.[19] The problem is not that such thought offers no illuminating insights for advanced capitalist societies or for the growing socialist movement. The problem is that the classic forms of Christian social organization are losing ground under the impact of modern societal forces. Thus, church and sect are giving way to a highly individualized, inward piety which lacks associational ties and institutional structures. Such piety is incapable of sustaining a Christian orientation to meaning and value. Troeltsch labeled this piety the "mystical type" of religious awareness, contrasting it with church and sect. He saw in it the disintegrating individualism of modern society. In response to this situation, Troeltsch increasingly shifted his attention away from Christian ethics as such to the critical possibilities of the civilizational ethic of European culture broadly conceived.[20] Not a few among us are moving in a similar direction.

Troeltsch's analysis can, however, equally well lead to renewed interest in the church as the ecclesial context of Christian ethics, not to the neglect of the civilizational ethic of contemporary societies, but as the social locus of their critical counterpoint. To be sure, such a counterpoint is not likely to be interesting to us so long as the dominant civilizational ethic appears viable and furnishes significant resources for dealing with contemporary social problems. In this respect, attempts to retrieve and appropriate Christian perspectives on the moral life have natural affinities with the various expressions of ethos criticism. They reflect a deep sense of the insufficiency of the normative understandings which currently provide direction for the basic institutions of society.

19. Ibid. p. 1011.
20. See Troeltsch's discussion of "Europaeismus" in *Der Historismus und seine Probleme* (1922), *Gesammelte Schriften,* III (Aalen: Scientia Verlag, 1966), pp. 703–18.

The way into a Christian critique of ethos, I would suggest, is through eschatology.[21] Christian faith is essentially eschatological. It consists of participation in the concrete reality of the coming new age in the midst of the persisting dominion of the old. As persons of faith, we cannot ignore or avoid the old age and its social forms, for it is yet too powerful. At the same time, we need not and may not any longer be awed by the symbols of authority it celebrates nor intimidated by its means of social control. It is an age which is passing away. We are already summoned to work out new ways of being together as human beings in the presence of the unfolding purposes of God. Our primary vocation is to become an eschatological community and to attest its promise for the world. Only out of the experience of eschatological existence are we in a position to determine appropriate ways of dealing with social institutions which continue to be subject to the organizational principles of the old age.

A distinctively Christian ethic has its social location in eschatological community. It is in such community that the Christian ethos is sustained, nurtured, and continually renewed. MacIntyre almost has it right: Christian thinking about ethics presupposes a Christian frame of reference. Yet an eschatological orientation is by no means closed, nor can it finally be described as circular. It is the orientation of a pilgrim people struggling in the midst of a hostile environment to enter into the reality of a new order of the world. Its logic is dialectical rather than syllogistic, which means it remains ever open to new discoveries and formations in the concrete interactions which are the stuff of history. Its basic structure is better represented by an open horizon than a circle.

Not content merely to protect and maintain a peculiar sub-culture, the reach of eschatological community is toward the whole inhabited earth.[22] Its aim is not the conversion of all peoples to an established point of view, but the negotiation of shared understandings capable of giving rise to a common world among women and men from a multiplicity of backgrounds and cultures. Its summons is to be a people in freedom and community, not apart from but precisely in relation to our social and cultural origins. Its vision is radically egalitarian, acknowledging no distinctions of race, ethnicity, sexual identity, or social function. Its bases of order are mercy and mutual forgiveness, eschewing violence and transcending adversarial combat. Its modes of social inter-

---

21. I have elaborated this theme in *The Use of the Bible in Christian Ethics* (Philadelphia: Fortress Press, 1983), pp. 177–94.

22. Some of the key motifs in an eschatological ethic are isolated in my study, "The Eschatological Horizon of New Testament Social Thought," *The Annual of the Society of Christian Ethics, 1983* (Waterloo, Ontario: Council on Study of Religion, 1983), pp. 55–80. [These key motifs are also elaborated in the final chapter of my book *Hospitality to the Stranger: Dimensions of Moral Understanding* (Philadelphia: Fortress Press, 1985), pp. 127–49, now available in an on-demand format by Westminster John Knox Press.]

action are patience and forebearance, resisting parochial arrogance and prideful self-exaltation at the expense of others. Its material foundations are caught up in patterns of social solidarity, a readiness to share the world's resources and to bear one another's burdens.

These notions cannot engage the civilizational ethic of contemporary societies without considerable development. That development, moreover, cannot occur apart from concrete social practice, specific attempts to build up human communities which embody their promise. Yet it is only by nurturing understandings of this sort in an ecclesial context that we can equip ourselves to make a Christian contribution to the social thought of our time. Troeltsch's analysis indicates that a Christian contribution to social thought can only become effective as part of a "compromise," a creative synthesis of Christian insights and the civilizational ethic of the age. Any compromise we might be able to achieve will be provisional, bound in its significance to a given phase of historical process. Nonetheless, participating in a dialectic which presses toward a creative compromise is at the heart of eschatological existence. We are called to be a pilgrim people, captured by a universal vision, moving steadfastly through an ambiguous and uncertain world.

Qty	Location	Item / ISBN / UPC	Condition	Price
1	A4-M18 - 001 - 00037 - 28747	The World Calling: The Church's Witness in Politics and Society [Paperback] by 0664228747	NEW	$19.75

Subtotal $19.75
Shipping $3.49
Total $23.24

YOUR ORDER HAS BEEN PAID IN FULL, NO FURTHER PAYMENT IS NECESSARY

BargainBookStores.com accepts returns within 30 days of order receipt. Please contact us before returning your order. Returns without prior authorization will not be refunded.

If you have any questions or concerns regarding this order, please contact us at: amazon@bargainbookstores.com

Thank you for purchasing from BargainBookStores.com!

BargainBookStores.com

Why Pay More?

4630 Danvers Drive SE

Grand Rapids, MI 49512

Customer Service Phone: 616-301-2349

Email: amazon@bargainbookstores.com

Tuesday, June 07, 2005

PAYMENT RECEIPT

Order Number:	AMZ299777
Ship Method:	**standard**
Customer Name:	Paul Collier
Order Date:	6/7/2005 7:47:24 AM
Seller Order:	058-7737494-9608556
Email:	collier@hickorytech.net

BargainBookStores.com

4630 Danvers Drive SE
Grand Rapids, MI 49512

TO:

Paul Collier
131 Moreland Ave

Mankato , MN , 56001-2278
United States